Sarah Stanley Grimké Collected Works

Personified Unthinkables (1884)

First Lessons in Reality (1886)

A Tour Through the Zodiac (1900)

K. Paul Johnson, Editor

TABLE OF CONTENTS

Foreword 7

Pupil 9

Personified Unthinkables 19

Teacher 45

First Lessons in Reality 65

Collaborator 117

A Tour Through the Zodiac 129

Appendices 175

Acknowledgments 193

Endnotes 195

Foreword

Sarah Stanley Grimké's only book was published two years after her death, without a word of explanation about the author's life and ideas. It includes two short works published during her lifetime and one longer work that first appeared in *Esoteric Lessons* in 1900. Astro-Philosophical Publications of Denver was the publishing arm of the Hermetic Brotherhood of Luxor [HBL], and *Esoteric Lessons* was overshadowed by the organization's major text, *The Light of Egypt*, published the same year in a newly expanded two volume edition. The 1889 one volume edition of *The Light of Egypt* was published under the pseudonym Zanoni, which in 1900 was linked to Thomas H. Burgoyne, alleged to have died in 1894. The publishers provided no more information about Burgoyne than about Grimké, and both have remained enigmatic ever since. For the historical detective Grimké is even more elusive in some ways than Burgoyne, and the circumstances of their collaboration remain mysterious despite years of research. Both of their lives during this period are shrouded in mystery, and their writings provide few clues to the historian. Published by a secret society, this book is also the work of a secretive author or authors.

Although *Esoteric Lessons* is written in the first person, its narrative is devoid of personal attributes and refers neither to individuals nor groups. The purely philosophical tone reveals its author only in terms of her abstract ideas. *The Light of Egypt*, by contrast, is somewhat more historically revealing about Burgoyne and the HBL. Only with the 1995 publication of the compilation *The Hermetic Brotherhood of Luxor* was much known about the order's founders in England and its history in France. The recently published correspondence of Thomas M. Johnson, the Brotherhood's Council President in the US during the mid-1880s, provides the first detailed portrait of its American membership. This annotated edition of *Esoteric Lessons* is intended as a companion to the Johnson correspondence, which provides the context in which Grimké was published. A letter from Burgoyne to Johnson reveals that soon after Grimké joined the Brotherhood in 1886, her published works became required reading for all members. However, they are purely a product of her interests in Mind Cure and Transcendentalism prior to affiliation with the HBL; only the third treatise in this book was written during her neo-Hermeticist phase.

Sarah's publications first appeared as a collection in 1900 entitled *Esoteric Lessons* and published the same year as a new two volume edition of *The Light of Egypt*. Because both of those 1900 collections obscured the lives of the authors more than revealing them, this new expanded collection is entitled *Sarah Stanley Grimké Collected Works*.

Pupil

Sarah Eliza Stanley was born in Scriba, Oswego County, New York in April 1850, the first year of her father's career as a Free Baptist clergyman. The following year Moses Stanley became pastor of a Free Baptist church in Fond du Lac, Wisconsin; in 1855 he returned to New England to another Free Baptist church in Farmington, Maine, a few miles from Wilton where his wife Sarah Pease Stanley had been born in 1827. In 1859 Moses was in Two Rivers, Wisconsin as pastor of a Congregational church, and beginning in 1860 he served Episcopal churches in Michigan and Indiana. In the first ten years of her life, Sarah thus lived in four states with a father affiliated with three denominations. Throughout her life, she formed no stable attachments to any place she could call home nor any Christian denomination, which was foreshadowed in her early childhood. The geographical and spiritual mobility of Moses Stanley's clerical career was reflected in his daughter's career as a writer. Another connecting thread for decades was abolitionism. The Free Baptist movement had begun in 1780 in New Hampshire, with the name referring to belief in free will as opposed to determinism. By the 1850s, "Free" for northern Baptists also referred to the divine imperative to end slavery. This denomination in which Sarah Stanley spent her early childhood had been strongly abolitionist, and Moses Stanley's commitment to the abolitionist cause continued into his Congregational and Episcopal pastorates. Sarah by marriage became a part of the most renowned abolitionist family of the 19th century.

Sarah Stanley graduated from Boston University, with a Ph.B. awarded by the College of Liberal Arts. Her Senior class of 1878 included twelve women and fifteen men. The "Philosophical course" leading to the Ph.B. Degree was discontinued upon their graduation of the class of 1880. Admission requirements for the College of Liberal Arts were daunting by modern standards, with Preliminary Examinations involving Greek and Latin Grammar and literature, Arithmetic, Algebra, English Grammar and Rhetoric, Modern History and Geography. Required Philosophy courses for all students included Theistic Philosophy, Ethical Philosophy, Evidences of Christianity, and History of Philosophy. Electives in Philosophy included Metaphysics, Logic and Theory of Knowledge, and Aesthetics. All philosophy courses were taught by Borden P. Bowne, remembered today as one of the foremost proponents of Personalism, a theistic Christian philosophy emphasizing the immanence of God. Bowne identified himself as a Berkeleyan idealist modified by Kantian epistemology. He taught psychology as well as philosophy, and published books on all major branches of philosophy as well as on theology.[1] In an obituary for the *American Journal of Theology*, John Alfred Faulkner lamented Bowne as a "severe loss not only to Boston University and American Methodism...but to American philosophy and theology and well" whose "writings cover almost every important branch of philosophy."[2]

Sarah converted to Unitarianism in Boston and was strongly influenced by the Transcendentalist Unitarian clergyman Cyrus Augustus Bartol. In April 1879 Bartol presided at her wedding ceremony when she married Archibald Henry Grimké, a native South Carolinian and the eldest of three sons of a white plantation owner and his enslaved mistress. Sarah's letters home announcing her engagement have not survived, but her father's reply dated February 21, 1879 is preserved in the Moorland-Spingarn Center at Howard University. He blamed both Bartol and her prospective in-laws for the engagement:

> There is not one of us who finds any pleasure in what seems to elate you. It may be a source of fun to the Unitarians of Boston but it has filled our hearts with mourning. You speak of the delight of Dr. Bartol and others. Do you think they would find the same delight if it were one of their daughters? We look upon it as a sad day when you went to Boston and especially when you associated yourself with the deniers of Christ and the insane theorizers of that infidel city. Boston will nevermore have any charms for me. We have always prided ourselves in you, but we are sorely, sorely

disappointed. You seem to have lost your reason—deceived by the Weld[s] and the delusive theorizers of the sickly and pestilent sentimentality of Boston. They are not your true friends who urge you on to this cause.[3]

Moses Stanley's dismay at his daughter's associates in Boston might be explained as a consequence of his earlier faith that she was in respectable company there in terms of Christian orthodoxy. Boston University's philosophy program was strongly theistic and influenced by the Methodist affiliation of the institution. Sarah's first year of philosophy education at the University of Michigan, in 1872-73 prior to her transfer to BU, was in a department led by another Methodist theologian, Benjamin Franklin Crocker. Hence her conversion to Unitarianism and abandonment of orthodox Christian theism would have been as shocking to her father as her interracial marriage.

Cyrus Bartol was one of the founding teachers of the Concord School of Philosophy. As pastor of West Church in Boston from 1837, and sole pastor from 1861 through retirement in 1889, he was the most visible exponent of Transcendentalism in the city in a career spanning five decades. Although Archibald Grimké was a resident of Boston and recent graduate of Harvard Law School, his aunt, uncle and cousins lived in Hyde Park where they were founding members of the Unitarian congregation. By referring to "the Weld," Moses Stanley accused his future son-in-law's white relatives of encouraging the marriage for ideological reasons. When Sarah Stanley married Archibald Grimké she took the surname of the most celebrated abolitionist women of the 19th century. Theodore Weld, like his wife Angelina Grimké Weld and her sister Sarah Moore Grimké, had begun as a traditional Protestant and passed through many phases of belief before finding a spiritual home among Unitarians in Hyde Park. The Grimké sisters' spiritual beliefs had inspired their long careers as abolitionist speakers and writers. Sarah Moore Grimké's dedication to the anti-slavery cause emerged after an 1823 conversion to Quakerism following several visits to Philadelphia. Angelina followed suit eight years later, both in joining the Friends and in support for abolitionists. Later they both developed an interest in Spiritualism, but ended life as Unitarians as did Theodore, who also in his final years embraced "mind cure."

Sarah Moore Grimké died in 1873 before Sarah Stanley went to Boston University; Angelina Grimké Weld had suffered a stroke the same year and died in 1879. They had discovered their nephews Archibald and Francis, biracial sons of their brother Henry, in 1868, and assisted their educational advancement in Massachusetts. Neither of the famed sisters could have been a direct influence on young Sarah, but Angelina's husband Theodore Weld was a definite presence in her family life. In his twenties, Theodore became a fervent apostle of the abolitionist cause, and early in his career he encountered the accusation that abolition of slavery would lead to race mixing, described by his biographer Robert Abzug as "one word, amalgamation, which was code for the mixing of the races."[4] Thinking of himself "as the John the Baptist of the antislavery movement," Weld had worked closely with free blacks for decades.[5] When young Archibald first encountered his aunts Sarah and Angelina, Weld fully supported their embrace of him and his brothers as family members. Abzug writes that Theodore "viewed the discovery of Archibald and Francis as the completion of the fateful union he had entered into so many years before with Angelina, coupling the destiny of the Weld family forever with that of the Grimkés—the black Grimkés—of Charleston...a chance, finally, to put into practice what they had all been preaching for so long."[6]

After the death of his wife, Theodore Weld, head of the extended Weld-Grimké clan, was a respected figure in his community. Mark Perry's history of the family depicts him in the early 1880s "walking slowly, on the arm of Sarah Stanley Grimké, through the streets of Hyde Park, where he had once jogged."[7] A 1925 biography of Archibald by his daughter describes the thrilling social network into which he was introduced by his aunts and Theodore Weld: "He met the Fosters, Lucy Stone, the famous Miss

Elizabeth Peabody, his old friends the Pillsburys, Judge Sewell, Dr. Bartol, Garrison, Sumner and Phillips, prominent and great men of his own race, such as Lewis Auden and Frederick Douglass."[8]

This was the world into which Sarah married in 1879. Child of an abolitionist minister, Sarah Stanley was fifteen years old at the end of the Civil War, and at twenty-nine she married a former slave. Themes of warfare and freeing slaves feature in her lessons written in the postwar era. Although her father Moses Stanley appears as her adversary at the time of her marriage, his moral evolution is apparent in his letters over the next two decades. He immediately saw "amalgamation" as an inevitable consequence, as Theodore Weld had insisted for decades, of abolishing slavery:

> It is what has been flung at me scores & perhaps hundreds of times in years past when I have advocated the rights of the colored race but little did I dream it was an arrow that would pierce my heart. I have advocated every measure for their full enfranchisement to civil & religious liberty & the opening of our schools & colleges for their education & culture, but amalgamation always seemed unnatural & revolting. Toward them I cherish none but philanthropic feelings but to give them my beautiful & accomplished daughter seems perfectly abhorrent, and that they should be willing to throw themselves into their arms for husbands is an infinite surprise & grief. The very thought of it is withering to all the love, the charm, the ambition, the aspiration of life. Death seems the only relief. I am ready to welcome death.[9]

Despite the hard feelings Moses Stanley expressed towards Sarah's conversion to Unitarianism in Boston and her marriage to Archibald, her geographical and spiritual mobility seems to follow his example. She moved from Transcendentalism to New Thought to Hermetic astrology, from Massachusetts to Michigan to California, with the same freedom that Moses had demonstrated in his life. Religious and geographical mobility is thus a theme connecting the Stanley and Weld/Grimké families.

The marriage had begun with a great intensity of feeling on both sides, as evident from this May 29, 1879 letter from Sarah to Archibald:

"Love! Lord! ay===Husband!
Art thou gone so?" And where am I? – I cannot tell who I am, nor what I should be doing here. I no longer have a separate being. My soul has gone and only a dull machine moves about – these rooms or the streets and commons of Boston. All is an unmeaning haze until my Prince return and revivify with his breath and magic touch...The Moral Education Society meeting this morning was very interesting indeed. Mrs. Woolson presided, and made a speech. Among the other speakers were Dr. Bartol, Rev. Mr. Withers, Mr. Allcott, &c – I met Miss Eddy on my way there so we were together.[10] (*Allcott is Bronson Alcott; "Miss" Eddy is Mary Baker Eddy- ed.*)

In this passage we find the best available clue in her letters to the combination of influences behind Sarah's earliest writings. Her correspondence only refers once to Bronson Alcott and Mary Baker Eddy, but many times to Cyrus Bartol, a recurring presence throughout her married life. Moses Stanley, in response to Sarah's announcement of her impending marriage, denounced Bartol's "delight" at the prospect of her marrying Archie. After leaving him in 1883, Sarah mentioned Bartol and his wife as the only Boston acquaintances with whom she wished to remain in contact. The triangular configuration of Alcott, Eddy, and Bartol provides the context in which Sarah, a Unitarian, became a Mind Cure author and later an exponent of Hermetic and Neoplatonic esotericism.

Bronson Alcott's acquaintance with Mary Baker Glover (who would become Mrs. Eddy in 1878) began when he read *Science and Health* in January 1876 and wrote to her in very admiring terms: "The sacred truths which you announce sustained by facts of the Immortal Life, give to your work the seal of inspiration – reaffirm, in modern phrase, the Christian revelations." [11] On January 30, after meeting Mrs. Glover, he wanted to meet her circle. He had already promoted her book among Transcendentalist colleagues and was planning to do so among future Unitarian clergy, writing "Last Sunday evening I met a pleasant circle at Mr Emersons and took occasion to speak of yourself, your Science and disciples...Next Wednesday evening, I am to meet the Divinity students at Cambridge for Conversation on Divine Ideas and methods. I think you may safely trust my commendations of your faith and methods anywhere."[12]After meeting her circle in Lynn, Alcott continued to be supportive. Three diary entries indicate the rise and fall of Alcott's enthusiasm for Christian Science. On January 20, 1876 he wrote "I find her one of the fair saints."[13] More than two years later, following the death of Mrs. Alcott and the remarriage of Mrs. Glover to Asa Gilbert Eddy, he became involved in a court case involving Christian Science, sometimes called the "Salem witch trial" of Daniel Spofford. Alcott's diary entry for May 14, 1878 notes that he accompanied Mr. and Mrs. Eddy to Salem for the trial in which Lucretia Brown claimed to have suffered mesmeric attacks from Spofford.[14] Three weeks later, on June 5, his first reservations about her appear in his diary: "There is perhaps a touch of fanaticism, though of a genial quality, interposed into her faith, which a deeper insight into the mysteries of life may ultimately remove."[15]

One sermon at Old West Church in which Cyrus Bartol endorsed Eddy's beliefs was entitled "Mind Cure." An excerpt was published in the *Christian Science Journal*, which included these passages: "A wrong thought disturbs right thinking. Rectify the system with right thoughts. That is the medicine to be taken internally...let us change the thought to faith, confidence in God, and in each other! Take down the upholstery of the pit. In a picture gallery we uncover our heads and are lifted above base longing. Can we not have an art museum in our mind? And spiritual uncovering."[16] At the Massachusetts Metaphysical College, May 7, 1884, the Christian Scientist Association members passed a resolution tendering "heartfelt thanks" to "this eminent divine" for having "nobly defended" Christian Science, concluding "as a true watchman on the tower of the world's progress who sends forth no uncertain sound do we thank him." [17]

References to Sarah in the literature of the time are rare, but in 1919 Horatio Dresser recorded her as "one of the earliest of the mental science writers" whose *Personified Unthinkables, 1884,* interpreted the practical idealism with special reference to mental pictures and their influence...Quimby sometimes described the mental part of his treatment with reference to the pictures he discerned intuitively in the patient's mind..."[18] The influence from Quimby on Grimké's writings may be minor, however, in light of the insistence of Cyrus Bartol on the same theme of mental pictures. Bartol became but the most visible friend of Christian Science in the Unitarian clergy. Stephen Gottschalk describes his interest in Eddy as based on "his feeling that the new movement represented a recrudescence of the Transcendentalist revolt against materialism."[19] He was not Mrs. Eddy's first Unitarian clerical admirer, a role played by Andrew Ralston Peabody, a Harvard professor affiliated with the orthodox Unitarians. Bartol was by contrast affiliated with the radical wing of the movement, in which "his liberalism partook not of the rationalism of Peabody's orthodoxy but of the warmth of transcendentalist faith."[20] Robert Peel notes in *Christian Science* an intriguing quote from Bartol, who allegedly "listened to Mrs. Eddy's explanations and declared, `I have preached the living God for forty years, but never felt his presence and power as you do.'"[21] Historian of Transcendentalism Philip Gura describes Bartol as "as a voice of postwar Transcendentalism" who was such "in good measure because of his continuing advocacy of intuitionist beliefs... became a major voice among radical Unitarians."[22]

An undated note by Calvin Frye of a recollection by Mary Baker Eddy, headed "Dr. Bartol- 1868," quotes him as telling her "Well dear sister I can see that you are inspired and your talk about God is beautiful but I cannot <quite>understand it I am afraid others will not I would not try to talk it for people will think you are insane."[23] This indicates that their acquaintance predated her first meeting with Bronson Alcott by eight years. Despite Eddy's early and lasting esteem for Bartol, the *Christian Science Journal* in December 1884 rejected his pleas for harmonious cooperation among various branches of the fractious Mind Cure movement. "Observer" commented that "There is no occupant of a Boston pulpit broader in his religious sympathies, or more sensitive in his spiritual fellowship, than the Rev. Dr. C.A. Bartol" who "has always been foremost in the recognition of ecclesiastical progress" and goes on to praise the way "every topic he touches receives from his thought a touch of its own poetic sweetness and light, yet not in such a way as to conceal or warp, in the least degree, the objects upon which he bids us look." Nevertheless, in a recent sermon Bartol went too far, when he classed Christian Science "with Mesmerism, Mind cure, Spiritualism, as parts of one and the same great movement...When Dr. Bartol, in his kindly way, bids Christian Scientists live in friendly unity with these isms, he asks the impossible."[24]

The mental pictures theme found in Grimké's writing, as well as her literary style, may owe more to Bartol than to Christian Science. His 1855 collection of sermons, *Pictures of Europe, Framed in Ideas*, combined travel writing and Transcendentalism. Sally M. Promey describes the book as inviting "'pilgrims' to the 'shrine,' the 'splendid temple of art'" and recommending "what he called 'picture-language' as superior to text for its presumed universal legibility."[25] The *Columbia Literary History of the United States* describes Bartol's style as "strongly didactic, much given to reflection on moral and spiritual truths, aphoristic, dependent on example and analogy rather than on sequential arguments, fond of paradox, highly reiterative yet sometimes compressed to the point of mysteriousness." [26] The *Esoteric Lessons* of his disciple are equally well described by this summary. The *Cambridge American Companion to Travel Writing* describes his 1855 book as "affirming the value of a universal religious reverence inherent in human nature and expressed in religious art and architecture."[27] The Sunday school lesson and sermon topics of Old West Church preserved at the Andover Theological Seminary library reveal Bartol emphasizing such visual themes as "The Beauty of Flowers" or "Light" as often as traditional Biblical topics or contemporary political issues.

One early critical Eddy biography describes her as presenting theology "warmer than the Unitarianism which it faintly resembled, less vague than the Transcendentalism with which it was affiliated."[28] Unitarian clergyman Samuel B. Stewart performed the marriage ceremony of Asa Eddy and Mary Baker Glover, who had attended his services with her former colleague Richard Kennedy.[29] Near the end of her long life, several pieces of evidence suggest that Eddy's early esteem for Unitarianism was undiminished. In November 1897, in response to an interview request from a Unitarian minister, she commented that "to my apprehension unity and love are the exemplification of Unitarianism, even as the Christ healing is the demonstration of Christian Science," adding "My acquaintance with Unitarians has been of a happy sort for their lives have illustrated their religion."[30] Six months later, she followed up with another letter praising several Unitarian clergymen by name, writing that "Theodore Parker, Dr. Peabody, Dr. Bartol, Wm. R. Alger, etc. were my model men. They did much towards unchaining the limbs of Love and giving freedom to its footsteps."[31] In recognition of years of friendly relations with the Unitarian Church in Concord, New Hampshire, Eddy left them $5000 in her will.[32] Two points in Unitarian theology are identified by Catherine Tumber as foundational to Christian Science, New Thought, and ultimately the New Age. Drawing on a philosophical tradition of perfectionism, "Unitarianism compelled its followers to achieve `likeness to God' through self-development and social reform" which was combined with a "precarious dualism between the higher and lower faculties, between the spiritual and the corporeal" which "could easily elide from respect for material claims, if legitimate in their proper inferior place, to active disparagement and even contempt."[33]

PERSONIFIED UNTHINKABLES

INTRODUCTION

It is certainly a self-evident proposition that actions can have *moral* quality only on a supposition of freedom.

It is also equally certain (though perhaps not so self-evident) that freedom is an absolutely necessary postulate of intelligence; for without the power of choosing an end or law and governing one's self accordingly, there could be no intellectual life. (Bowne's Metaphysics, pages 168-169)[34]

But that health — so called physical health — is possible *only* through the fact of freedom, will *probably*, appear to most minds as a *self-evident absurdity*.

The *connection* between Body, Intellect and Morals, no one denies. But it has been generally accepted on the authority of materialistic science.

Physiology measures out our intellectual life for us, and even goes so far as to decide the extent of *moral responsibility* from the structure of the brain. While the thorough-going Materialist affirms that the Mechanism is sufficient to explain all the phenomena of *Will*, even going so far as to calmly suggest as a recent writer (Maudsley's Body and Will, page 82)[35] does, that desire for suicide, for immortality, annihilation, etc., are severally the necessary *result* of the state of the body in which the individual had no choosing.

This pushes the whole subject to an issue on the question of free will.

The moralist and intellectualist can no longer assert Freedom, while they leave *Health* to be explained by the mechanism; for they are thus still at the mercy of the materialist. Philosophy, both Ethical and Theistic, in defending itself against materialism, has quite overlooked this fact.

Health has been recognized only as an important conditioning physical fact. But a spiritual philosophy, (whether it be Idealism or Phenomenalism), which regards physical manifestations as entirely, or in any degree a product or effect of *Mind*, must no longer *theoretically* or *practically* exempt Body.

Body in all its varying manifestations must be *effect* or *result* of *Thought*.

The basis of Health must be wholly mental, and it follows directly from this that the basis of Disease must likewise be wholly mental.

Disease and Evil must both be the direct and indirect results of an *erroneous judgement*. Here the materialist would stoutly affirm that the erroneous judgement was the necessary result of the state of the *body*, in which the individual had no *choosing*.

And here the spiritual philosopher must as stoutly affirm that all so-called diseases of Body are simply effects of a mental cause, the necessary result of an *error of reason*, and that mind does have the power of correcting its own mistakes of judgment.

But the possibility of forming an erroneous judgment, and the power of correcting it, *both* imply Freedom.

The fact of Freedom does not by any manner of means make an ignorant man learned by the simple choosing.

It does not make an evil man virtuous, without some effort on his part; nor does it lift the sick man from his bed, to simply choose to be well.

But when reason tells me that two plus two equals four, if I choose to turn round and say perhaps after all two plus two equals five, I exercise my freedom in the matter. I do not alter the *Truth*, but as far as the *moral* or *physical* effects upon myself are concerned I can change results. I can realize the *Truth*, or I can realize the effects of a denial of the *Truth*.

By Freedom, either for the individual or the race, is simply meant a power to choose some *Truth* or its *Contradictory*; some *Reality* or its opposite *Nothingness*, and to regulate one's self accordingly.

If any one should affirm that effects could exist without any cause whatsoever, he would but *illustrate* the possibility of saying a thing was so, when it was NOT so.

Further, if any one should accept this statement as so, which was not so, and should regulate his actions accordingly he would certainly realize results in accordance with his erroneous judgment.

Now the *Reality* of a *feeling* consists in being *felt*. Yet the foundation of the feeling may be perfectly false. The feeling may be wholly the *result* of the possibility of saying a thing is so when it is not so.

Thus persons have been known to lose the power of speech and motion, to fall fainting and *lifeless* even, upon a *false* alarm of fire in a building.

No fire at all; still the feeling of fear and its results upon the body were real enough while they lasted.

All these *results* were from a belief in a lie.

But if mind is endowed with trustworthy faculties for ascertaining the truth or falsity of a *report*, and mind does not *choose* to exercise them, is not that mind in a measure responsible for its own sufferings?

A different state of mind would certainly change results completely.

The same person who falls imbecile or lifeless, upon a false alarm of fire, if inspired by perfect *fearlessness*, or a touch of heroism, could pass unharmed through *raging flames.*

Now if a person chooses to believe a false alarm of fire, *that does not make a fire, when there is none.* It does not make a Reality out of Nothing. Such persons only *change results* as far as they themselves are concerned.

If then all the Reality, commonly called *purely corporeal diseases,* possess, can be shown to be the RESULT of the possibility of saying, or believing a thing is so when it is NOT SO, that would establish Disease to be the result of an erroneous judgment; and since the possibility of forming an erroneous judgment implies (1) Freedom; (2) that there is *absolute truth of Reason,* (Bowne's Metaphysics, page 168)[36]— that would also at the same time establish HEALTH to be *wisdom, knowledge, insight.* Thus would our new Doctrine of Health be demonstrated. For Health would be *Wisdom* if Disease was lack of Wisdom. Now if *Physical Causation* is as false as a false alarm of fire, any one who affirms Physical Causation but illustrates the possibility of saying a thing is so when it is NOT so.[37]

If the *individual* or the *race* accept Physical Causation as true and regulate themselves accordingly, they are certain to realize *Results* in accordance with the erroneous judgment of Physical Causation.

In Logic the Law of Contradictories is called a *fundamental Law of thought.* According to this Law, "One of two contradictories *must* be affirmed." It would, for example, be a violation of this Law to affirm, that *all* right angles are equal, and at the same time assert that *some* right angles were larger than others.

Our aim is to deduce this doctrine of Health from Theistic or Spiritual Philosophy; and to point out that Theistic Philosophy cannot affirm Physical Causation, even in the case of so-called purely corporeal diseases, without a self-evident violation of the Law of Contradictories.

PART I.

REALITY.

AN OUTLINE STATEMENT OF HOW ALL REALITY IS TO BE REGARDED.

The Absolute; the Unknowable; the Infinite Essence; First Cause, etc., are some of the fashionable terms employed to denote our concept of the Supreme Reality of the Universe.

They have the praiseworthy quality of being quite unpicturable; but their unpicturability results rather more from their lack of meaning than anything else.

The terms Being, Reality, Infinite, etc., are logical abstractions in themselves, and have no real meaning apart from some active agent. But in that connection they do have meaning.

Our highest conception of an active agent is the conscious ego, or Mind.

Now there is certainly nothing in the Universe so utterly unpicturable as Mind. What possible picture can one form of the part of him which reasons, reflects, gives judgments, forms decisions, etc. ?

Besides being unpicturable, the term Mind stands for the most definite, vivid and self-evident fact of consciousness.

Therefore Mind, our highest, most real, definite and knowable term for a Unitary Active Agent, we adopt for the present purpose, as the Source of all Reality in the Universe. Infinite Mind!

It is impossible to conceive of a mind without thoughts.

On the other hand, thoughts have no independent existence by themselves. They are not a community loafing around waiting for some Mind to think them. Neither are thoughts, mind, nor mind, thoughts. There is an ultimate dualism between the two. They can never lose their identity and change, the one to the other.

Yet mind implies thoughts. They cannot exist apart. They are therefore what may be called Real or Polar Opposites. They mutually imply each other.

Thought, or product of mind, regarded by itself is quite as unpicturable as mind. However, in connection with thought, occurs a phenomenon, the importance and significance of which, in all its bearings, perhaps, has not been sufficiently regarded by philosophy and psychology, viz : —

For every thought there is an accompanying mental picture of some kind. If the thing itself cannot be pictured, there will still be an accompanying mental picture of some manifestation or appearance of the thing.

If the idea triangle is called to mind, one cannot think of it without seeing in his "mind's eye" a figure with three sides. One cannot reflect upon so-called general ideas without a mental picture. Take e. g. the general term Animal. We find at once an accompanying mental picture of some individual included under the class, animal; e. g, a dog or lion, etc.

Neither can one consider ideas regarded abstractly, such as, Life, Love or Virtue, without some object possessing Life, Love or Virtue, picturing itself to the mind.

Furthermore these mental pictures either, (1) correspond to. previous sensations derived from phenomena or visible universe, or (2) they are original constructions made up out of previous sensations by means of association, comparison, etc.

Mental pictures are therefore, (1) the mind's symbols for objective phenomena, and (2) they are representations of the activities — the working over processes of intellect.

The first class, the finite ego, refers to some other agent than itself as cause, but the second it claims as its own construction.

Its images, or ideals, the finite mind is instinctively impelled to put in some form recognizable to the senses. ("Berkley affirmed an objective and spiritual ground of our sensations as an absolute necessity of thought. He questioned only the external existence of the object in perception, and reduced it to an effect in us.")[38]

To the Artist, the Poet, the Author, we accord our highest praise and admiration in proportion as they succeed in creating the most perfect form or expression for their ideals.

Mental images are then the mediation between unpicturable thought, and a representation to the senses, of thought.

They are the purely mental expression for the thoughts which the Artist puts on canvas, the Poet and the Author into form for eye and ear.

The creative faculty we regard as the highest mark of genius in finite mind.

But in the real, the ontological sense of the word Infinite Mind, is the only Creator. It is also, in the true sense of the word, the Only Mind in the Universe.

The finite mind stands in the relation of Thought to this One Great Mind.

(1.) Thoughts can never be the mind which thinks them. (2.) Again the sum of all the thoughts of Infinite Mind can never equal the One Mind. (3.) Again thought has no independent existence apart from mind. Therefore: (1.) Man can never be God. (2.) All mankind together can never equal God. (3.) Man is an utter unthinkability apart from God.

For every thought of Infinite Mind, there exists, so to speak, an accompanying mental picture, type or ideal. These types or ideals, the Idealist regards as the reality of Phenomena, or visible Universe.

Here the Idealists divide into two classes. Neither class denies that there is objective reality.

"Berkley affirmed an objective and spiritual ground of our sensations as an absolute necessity of thought. He questioned only the external existence of the object in perception, and reduced it to an effect in us." (Bowne's Metaphysics, page 451)

The other class regards the mental ideal or type as the reality of phenomena but also hold as Leibnitz did, that visible universe is a creative act. It is the ideal of thought realized in act.

Since whichever class may have the truth of the matter does not to any extent affect the present argument, visible universe is regarded as a Creation for the realization of a purpose; also as an expression of an ideal, just as an artist seeks to represent his ideals of thought.

But for all that, phenomenon is only an appearance. It has no more substance in it than the vivid reflections thrown upon a screen or wall by the magic lantern, which presents to the eye a perfect, beautiful and certainly a most real appearance.[39]

Just as every minutest detail of the brilliant picture on the wall corresponds to a small transparency within the lantern, just so phenomenon is the reflection of an ideal of Infinite Mind.

The reflection of a thought has no substance, (the words substance and matter ought to be annihilated) but it has reality.

Just as all the reality the reflection on the screen possesses is derived from the magic lantern, just so all the Reality of visible universe is derived from Infinite Mind consists in its purely mental quality.

Therefore as an act of Infinite Mind the reflection of a thought is real. For all the Divine doing is Real.

And all the Divine doing is perfect, beautiful, harmonious; perfect in Order, Health and Happiness. Whatever other appearance man may imagine he sees there is an entirely gratuitous contribution on his part. An example of the exercise of his freedom to form erroneous judgments, whereby he does not alter Truth or Reality; but merely as far as he himself is concerned, changes results.

All the Reality, then, in the Universe, is to be regarded as in a direct line from One Source. Also in a regular grade of order which cannot be reversed or worked backwards any more than, in the case of the magic lantern, the reflection can be the cause of the transparencies, or lenses — or again the transparencies or lenses can be the cause of the light in the lantern.

1. Infinite Mind.

2. Infinite Thoughts.

3. Infinite Ideals of Infinite Thoughts.

4. Infinite Expressions, or Ideals Realized in Act; — Visible Universe.

PART II.

POLAR OPPOSITES.

REAL OR POLAR OPPOSITES.

Infinite Mind.
Infinite Thoughts.

(Thought — Symbols.
(Unity — Multiplicity.
(Identity — Diversity.

Being.
Attributes.

Real or Polar Opposites are necessarily reciprocal. They do not *exclude*, but mutually imply each other. (Cocker's Handbook of Philosophy, Division I, p. 177)[40] They are utterly meaningless apart. One cannot exist without the other.

(1.) Thought and symbol are Polar Opposites just as much as Mind and Thoughts. They have no existence apart. Mind cannot think a thought without sign or symbol of some kind. The Thought for which mind has no mental conception, is perfectly meaningless. Mind has not thought it. If the senses have never given the symbol which mind has translated into the idea *Triangle*, or if Mind has never constructed it out of its previous sensation of lines and angles, that mind has never thought the idea Triangle.

(2.) The same thought may be expressed in a multiplicity of ways, as e. g. the idea Castle may be expressed by a *word* spoken or written, — by the architect on paper, by the mechanic in brick or stone, or by the artist on canvas, etc.

The Thought never loses its *Unity*, no matter how numerous the forms which represent it.

(3.) Again, the idea *Cube* never changes to the idea Cylinder; nor the idea Cylinder to the idea Sphere. Yet the form which expresses the idea *cube* assumes the exact appearance of the *form* cylinder by simply revolving the cube (suspended at the center of one of its sides), and a perfect sphere is produced as far as the sense of sight can inform us by rotating the cylinder (suspended at the center by its round side.) (Froebel's Kindergarten System. — The Second Gift.)[41]

Throughout the phenomenal universe, the idea remains forever the same. The idea *solid* does not change to the idea *liquid* nor the idea *liquid* into the idea *vapor*. Yet the appearance, or expression for the idea may change from one to the other right before our eyes, as in the case of water.

We cannot therefore affirm identity of phenomena. When we change ice into steam and then back into ice again, we cannot affirm that we have the *same* piece of ice with which we started. But thought can never lose its *identity* nor its *unity*, nor cease to *exist* as long as mind exists to think it. Therefore this Thought of Infinite Mind which you and I represent cannot cease to *exist*, nor lose its *unity* nor its *identity* any more than Infinite Mind can cease to exist, since Mind and Thoughts imply each other. Further, since Thought and Symbol are likewise polar opposites which imply each other, we shall always have *expression* or *body* of some kind or other.

Phenomenal universe of some kind must always exist, as long as Infinite Mind exists. We cannot blot out one and leave the other any more than by rubbing the vivid reflections thrown upon the wall by the magic lantern, we can erase the picture while the lantern continues to burn. Or any more than we can put the lantern out and still have our picture left on the wall.

(4.) *Pure* or *Absolute* BEING apart from Attributes is quite as unthinkable as Mind without Thoughts. Life, Truth, Virtue, in the abstract, are quite as meaningless and absurd as it would be to talk about a *smile* or a *grin* in the *abstract*, floating round in the air, or which no one had ever *smiled* or *grinned*.

Abstraction, however, is the first act or condition in knowledge. It is the withdrawal of attention to a part. (Cocker's Handbook of Philosophy, Division 1, p. 169.)

We have seen that all REALITY was to be regarded as in a direct *line* and *order* from the same Source. But the whole process of knowledge, however, follows along the *reversed line*; and thus (as we shall see) with *Abstraction*, or the first step in knowledge, has occurred *Personification*, or the fundamental error.

Attention (abstraction) is first directed to Phenomena. Sensations are *mental translations* of Phenomena. Sensations, again, are not *entities.* They are only Sensations as they are thought by mind; only as they are an *act* of the conscious ego. There are two ways, however, of regarding this one *act.* At the same time the ego recognizes its sensations as its own, it also recognizes that the sensations stand for something *not* its own; and thus arrives at phenomena. Here it observes most wonderful manifestations of power, law, truth, life, etc., etc., and is impressed with overwhelming Reality. Thus it is led to *personify* Nature, or endow Phenomena with *independent* Reality; not realizing the fact that *Visible Universe* is purely a mental expression of Thought, that if Infinite Mind could cease to exist, all the appearances which seem so *vast* and *everlasting*, would vanish like a bubble without leaving the *shadow of a dream behind.*

The ego having personified Nature, when it arrives at some knowledge of Infinite Mind has two opposing *Realities* in the universe —Mind and Matter — or if it has personified the various Laws, Forces, etc., which it *abstracted* on its way, it already has a host of Divinities.

Personification, then, is the fundamental lie, which has attended abstraction, — the first step in *knowledge*.[42]

Personification is from *persona*, the Latin word for a mask; and obtained its present significance from the fact that Actors were in the habit of wearing masks in the plays. That is, by means of masks they assumed to be personages they were not.

So the ego in turning its attention to phenomena, endowed the *manifestations* of Reality, with an independent existence and Reality which they do not possess. And thus *counted* the *mask*, (the *appearance*), for *One*, as well as the Actor, *One*, quite overlooking the fact that the Actor, and the *character* he *personates*, cannot count as *Two* distinct individuals.

When the ego comes to explain Body and Soul as the union of mind and matter, it has two irreconcilable forces. In proportion as matter is allowed dominion, Intellect and Morals are SLAVES, until in a final struggle for consistency, Matter is declared Omnipotent! Mind is but *reflection*, *expression* of MATTER. *Mechanism* is fully competent to explain all appearance or phenomena of mind.

Sensations are all.

John Stuart Mill asserts that, "In the language of philosophy, feelings and states of consciousness are synonymous; everything is a feeling of which the mind is conscious." (Logic," ch. III.) [43]

Although Mr. Mill establishes a scale of rank in feelings, yet such statements reduced to their lowest terms degrade Philosophy to some such gibberish as the following: — *Algo ten kephaten; ergo sum.* — I suffer a headache; therefore I exist. The Greek and Latin give an appearance of learning, but looking *behind the Mask*, at the content of the sentence, every healthy mind is instinctively impelled in the name of Philosophy to sledge-hammer it as a lie, and then start out once more with that lofty assertion of Des Cartes, "I think, therefore I *exist.*" And I *exist*, because Infinite Mind Thinks. And I have no *existence* apart from Infinite Mind. In that sense, "I and the Father are One."

The Law of Polar Opposites is the most fundamental law in the universe; and Personification is a direct and stupid violation of that law. Personification is Idolatry. (Book of Exodus, Chap. XX, verses 3 to 7.)[44]

PART III.

CONTRADICTORIES.

Truth.	Falsity
Virtue.	Evil
Health.	Disease
Life.	Death

The Law of Contradictories is a fundamental Law of Thought.[45] According to this law, "ONE of two contradictories *must be affirmed*."

All Contradictories of *universal, necessary* and *absolute* TRUTH are impossible; and UNTHINKABLE. (Cocker's Handbook of Philosophy, Division i, p. i.)[46]

On the opposite side of the great principles of Truth, Virtue, Health, Life, etc., the ego beholds another set of appearances which it also at once proceeds to *personify*, to establish as realities, viz. : Falsity, Evil, Disease and Death, until, however, gradually coming to comprehend there can be no such thing as attributes apart from Being, that Truth, Virtue, Health and Life, etc., are meaningless abstractions by themselves, it is confronted by the monstrous paralogism of affirming that if Falsity, Disease, Evil and Death are also Attributes of Being, are Realities, just as much as Truth, Virtue, Health and Life are Realities, then *Falsity, Evil, Disease and Death*, and Being are necessarily reciprocal. They do not exclude, but mutually imply each other.

Infinite Mind, and Falsity, Evil, Disease, and Death are utterly meaningless apart; one cannot exist without the other! And thus to avoid the revolting necessity of making the Infinite the *Father of Lies*, another (Personage) mask is introduced into the Universe to father this new set of Realities. A necessity which might have been wholly obviated by the correction of the very simple blunder in the premises, viz.: — that Falsity, Evil, Disease, and Death are not polar opposites of Being at all, they are the purely *Verbal Opposites*, or Contradictories of the ATTRIBUTES of Being.

What rational ground is there, then, for affirming them to be Realities, or the Attributes of Being? Is it not, on the other hand, a direct violation of the law of Contradictories to do so?

If we affirm the proposition; some right angles are larger than others, to be equally true with the proposition, all right angles are equal, we at once introduce confusion and chaos not only into mathematics, but also into Astronomy, Physics, or, in short all the Arts and Sciences depending on mathematics. So long as we maintain that single Falsity to be a Reality, just so long would we remain in the densest ignorance on all these subjects. We would not alter the Truth, but only as far as we ourselves are concerned, we would change results. Whether we will or no, we cannot *possibly* affirm both of two Contradictories. It we hold fast to one, we lose the other. And we must affirm TRUTH and deny its verbal opposite as an absolute UNTHINKABLE, in order to make the slightest advance in knowledge.

Now since all the Contradictories of universal, necessary and absolute Truth are impossible, are *Unthinkables*, we must either affirm Truth, Virtue, *Health* (from Anglo- Saxon hal, WHOLE), Life, Love, etc., to be universal, necessary and absolute Truths, and their contradictories unthinkables, or else we must affirm Falsity, Evil, Disease, Death, Hate, etc., to be universal, necessary and absolute truths and their contradictories unthinkables. A conclusion which the consistent Materialist accepts either openly or else practically.

But a conclusion the Spiritual Philosopher cannot accept without a most flagrant violation of the Law of Contradictories.

But here the ego immediately inquires: How, then, come these appearances which seem so real; take, e. g., the manifestations of Evil, the contradictory of Virtue?

Here, however, a moment's reflection convinces us, this class of manifestations we universally regard as *results*. Moral quality is never affirmed of results, but of the *thought* which actuated the results. To remove the results in no way affects the guilt of the Thought.

But again the ego questions: Why is not the *erroneous judgment* back of the results of Evil, as evidently unthinkable as the statement, some right angles are larger than others?

The answer is plain enough. It is purely a matter of insight, of education.

The race has been so accustomed to accept truth from authority instead of reason, that with most minds a college degree will outweigh any logical demonstration.

It is an *erroneous judgment* that self interest or happiness ever in any way conflict with Virtue.

On the *contrary*, the welfare and happiness of the individual, and of the race depend unconditionally upon Virtue.

It is just as untrue that a man is the slave of his senses, as that some right angles are larger than others. But, just as surely as a man comes to the conclusion that his senses rule him, or were given for personal gratification, just so surely the physical, or phenomenal results of such a decision begin to manifest themselves. And since *Intellect and the Senses meet through the imagining faculty*, Intellect having accepted the unthinkable, the impossible for Truth, for Reality, IMAGINATION proceeds to portray these Unthinkables to the senses. And all the acts of that man thereafter are *results* of that one mental error.

But, right here must be noticed an important and undeniable fact, viz.: The whole *physical* organization also responds to the mental error. A *momentary* thought of sensuality, avarice, or revenge, distorts the face, impairs respiration, retards or quickens the circulation, and goes tingling through every nerve and fibre of the body. But if long enough continued it results in either Disease of some form, or permanent deformity of the features, if not of the whole body, or both.

Very many forms of Disease are well known to be the results of immorality, and consequently purely mental origin. Yet it never seems to strike one as at all absurd to *physic* a man for Avarice, or Revenge. On the contrary it is taken for granted as the proper thing to do. Still the person who should undertake to remove an ugly image reflected on a wall by a magic lantern, with a coat of whitewash, would in all probability be regarded, either as *non compos mentis*, or, as a very great ignoramus. No matter how much one may try to ignore the fact, or cheat the senses, by hanging a dark curtain over the ugly picture, yet Reason will insist that the reflection is still there as long as the lantern remains intact; and that you have only to lift the dark curtain to be again confronted by the unseemly reflection. There is but one way to remove it from the wall, and that must be done by a change inside the *Lantern*.

In like manner as long as the mental image for an unthinkable is held in the mind, just so long- will the immoral results continue to manifest themselves.

But, just as surely as the erroneous judgment is *corrected*, all the results of the personified unthinkable will be replaced by manifestations of Truth, Pure living, and High thinking.

The complete reformation of an immoral man would not then be the miracle it now is, if *physical causation* were seen to be as utterly unthinkable, as for the *Reflections* of the magic lantern to be the *Cause* of the image they reflect.

But such results are impossible on a basis of physical necessity, and, moreover, as long as physical causation is allowed in the slightest degree, Morals are at the mercy of *Chance*. For a man may be free one moment but necessitated the next. Or again one man might be entirely free under circumstances which would render another wholly necessitated.

The fundamental lie, then, which opens the door to evil and which continues to hold it open is *physical causation*, or allowing the senses dictatorship. The office of the Senses is solely to report phenomena. Reason translates it into Knowledge. The Senses should give us neither pleasure nor pain. Either pleasure or pain denotes perversion of their use. In their office they should be as sensationless and unconscious as *perfect digestion*. The pleasure derived from the harmony of color or sound, or proportion should be wholly intellectual. Pain should be the revolt of the intellect against an untruth. For discord and inharmony are but expressions for a lie!

Pleasure and Pain are both results of the erroneous judgment of Physical Causation, for Physical Causation is as absolutely unthinkable as it would be for the reflections of the magic lantern to be the *Cause* of the Reality they reflect; or, for Thoughts to be the *Cause* of the Ego or Mind which thinks them.

This conclusion, however, being thoroughly contrary to established belief will not be readily accepted in the case of so-called purely physical Disease. For although mental and moral causation is generally conceded for a large class of bodily maladies, yet physical causation is insisted upon for a large proportion.

Feuchtersleben says: "The operations of body and mind meet in the fancy (or imagination) as in a *punctum saliens*; it is only through the imagination that they act and re-act together. *Thought without an image cannot become diseased; nor can sensations without imagination become psychically diseased.* Below imagination we find affections of the sensor and motor nerves which remain purely corporeal diseases so long as they do not encroach upon her domain." (*Medical Psychology*, pp. 241-242.)[47]

But how can they become diseased and not encroach upon her domain? For all our knowledge and experience of sensor and motor nerves is derived *wholly* from their diseased condition. No one would ever have known of nerves from their *healthy* condition. They never report themselves. But having become disordered they *do* report themselves; and the report must of *necessity* be made through the imagining faculty. There is no other way. The only point which remains then, to consider, is whether sensor and motor nerves get out of order themselves, or by some misuse on the part of the ego. If then, diseased conditions of sensor or motor nerves can be shown to be *results* of erroneous judgment, there certainly need no longer be any reason for the Spiritualistic Philosopher to violate the Law of Contradictories, even to the extent of affirming Physical Causation in the solitary case of sensor and motor nerves.

The true definition of CAUSE is: "Whatsoever WILL, does or DID DO." (Chas. De Medici, Commensuration, p. 12.)[48] Throughout the phenomenal Universe we observe only an orderly succession of events, never *Cause.* Our only experience of cause is when phenomena is modified through human agency or design. Thus man can combine Hydrogen and Oxygen in the *proportion* of two volumes of H to one of O and produce the result H_2O, or Water, through his own design and agency. But at the same time he is conscious that he is not the author of the *immutable principle* necessary to the combination, and instinctively concludes to a Supreme CAUSE or WILL, as an ultimate ground of all the orderly succession of events observable in the Universe. The finite ego is the immediate or efficient cause of change or modification of phenomena observable about us in human life. While the Infinite is the ultimate Cause of the immutable principles back of Visible Universe. Reason can never be satisfied with any causation apart from *Will*. Especially since it must necessarily result so disastrously to Intellect and Morals.

Simply because the senses report certain appearances followed by suffering and disorder of the Organism, which interfere with the functions of body and mind is not sufficient, reason for affirming Physical Causation in the case of purely corporeal Diseases. For, why should Reason allow the Senses to be competent to furnish the truth in this one case, while in every other the Senses but furnish the data which Reason alone is competent to work over into knowledge? The *Senses* would at this very moment, (if they were consulted), *insist* that the Earth is stationary; and *deny* point blank the fact that the earth is whirling through Space, in its Orbit, at the rate of 68,288 miles an hour.

If then a perfectly satisfactory explanation of all so-called purely corporeal diseases can be given by assuming *physical causation* to be the *erroneous judgment* which *results, either directly* or indirectly in corporeal diseases, Reason is bound to accept it, since it would thus forever dispose of both *Physical Causation* and *Corporeal Disease* by effectually *knocking* their heads together.

(1.) A belief in *physical causation* produces Fear, and Fear acts both directly and indirectly upon the body.[49] Often immediately upon the sensor and motor nerves in like manner as was seen in the illustration of the immediate results of Avarice and Revenge upon *sensor* and *motor* nerves; or in the case of the results observed upon a belief in a false alarm of fire. It would be impossible to dismay that mind which was in *conscious possession* of its perfect ability to subdue the fire, or else to escape from the flames uninjured. Especially if the consciousness of perfect ability was based upon the knowledge that the only conceivable danger would result from *Fear*. Just so perfect *fearlessness* has carried many untouched through the most violent contagions of cholera, small-pox, yellow fever, etc.

(2.) Fear is also the remote, or (latent) cause of disease, as a race belief held throughout the whole history of mankind. It is the *open door* through which the Enemy can at any moment rush in and bind the strong man. It is co-existent with the first Personified Abstraction, or the lie of an independent Reality apart from and hostile to Mind. Observe the "Fossil history' to be seen in the formation of the two words Health and Disease. Dis-ease is the lack of ease immediately resulting from the erroneous conceptions of an independent Health (anglo-saxon Hal. *Whole!*) Wholeness apart from Infinite Mind.

This one *lie* lurks behind a million different *Masks*, which pass for so many different entities and Realities. Every scientifically labelled Disease with its various attending symptoms minutely and vividly pictured out to the senses is a Mask. The *Lie* and its masks are Personae" of a *Stupendous Masquerade* under Personified Unthinkables. The "Dramatis the auspices of Materialism, and the stage management of Physical Causation. An High Carnival which might be sufficiently entertaining but for the fact that its swift and inevitable termination in that woeful TRAGEDY OF ERRORS — the Errors of Falsity, Evil, Disease and Death, touches a chord which vibrates in every [word missing in original]. Here the ego insists upon an answer to the human heart.

Question: *How* is it possible for a lie or an unthinkable to be expressed upon the body? But one answer is possible. It is manifested on the same principle as all Thought in the Universe; that grand principle according to which all REALITY is manifested; the immutable principle of which the finite is not the author and which it cannot alter, although it may deny. But if it *denies*, it reaps the results of the *denial* worked out on the very principle which it denies.

One can write out on a black-board the statement for the unthinkable two plus two equals five; he, there, has a manifestation of a lie. If he affirm the lie to be true and on the strength of the affirmation gets $5 out of his neighbor instead of $4 there are immediately, immoral results from the lie.

Now, Rheumatism or Pneumonia, etc., are *Verbal* expressions for unthinkables just as two plus two equals five is a verbal expression for a lie. By means of the picturing faculty, both of the individual and of those about him, the outward manifestation of the unthinkable will express itself upon the body just as surely as the magic lantern will reflect the picture inserted between the light and the lenses when the proper conditions are met.

This explanation reduces *all* physical phenomena in the Universe to the manifestation of Thought and removes the contradictory from the philosophy which affirms man to be the union of mind and matter, and the erroneous judgment that Soul and body interact. WILL is the only CAUSE in the Universe of which we have any knowledge or experience. That Will modifies, changes and controls the physical is our hourly and daily experience. But how matter, even in the form of sensor and motor nerves can change itself into sensations transcends all experience. On the other hand, mind can locate sensations in any part of the body at will. Thus cases are common (quite too common) where from the simple trimming of the finger nails some persons actually suffer more than others would from cutting into the skin. Again others pride themselves upon such an acute sense of digestion that they can tell the exact ingredients of their food even when the palate is deceived.

Soul and body cannot interact any more than the *Reflection* and the *Magic Lantern interact.*

Quinine or Physic never made a sick man well, any more than a dead man could double up his fist and strike a blow. Faith in the knowledge and skill of the doctor who prescribed the medicine; hopefulness in those about the sick man changes the mental image until the *appearance* of disease, like *Dissolving View*, fades into the glorious *Reality* of Health.

The problem of Health, then, would be how to cultivate and keep clean and healthy pictures in the mind. Health would then be an essential part of the ego. Man would be a strict unity not a trinity of Intellect, Body and Morals.

And the absolutely necessary postulates of this Unity would be Infinite Mind, Freedom and Eternal Life.

One more Contradictory remains to be considered, viz.: The Contradictory of Life. If we affirm life to be a universal, necessary and absolute Truth, then Death is impossible and unthinkable.

The appearance called death is therefore only the last stage of the Lie of Physical Causation in which the lie and its mask are swallowed up in the victory of Truth, in which the Personified Unthinkable is *erased* from off the boards of Reality.

Heaven is not a PLACE where there is no more sinning, suffering and dying. It is a state of *Intellectual development*. And when the finite reaches that stage of Insight by which the contradictories of all attributes of Infinite Mind are seen to be self-evident Unthinkables — *then* there will be no more death, no matter whether that degree of WISDOM is attained upon this Earth or in some other Sidereal System.

CONCLUSION.

A few more words remain to be said in regard to the *use* of the Verbal Opposite, or Contradictories. Since there is such a thing as Verbal Opposite, what is its office in our mental activities? Reason insists that nothing is useless or meaningless in the Universe. Why, then, is it possible to *say* or to *believe* a thing is *so* when it is not so?

Consider, then, for a moment, the proposition that two straight lines cannot enclose space. Nothing can make the truth of the proposition so manifest, as the attempt to think its contradictory, — (two straight lines CAN inclose space.) In fact, Truth cannot be *established* or proved in any other way. A truth is only accepted nominally or on trial, as it were, until its contradictory is seen to be a self-evident UNTHINKABLE. This principle of Contradictories is, then, our *Touchstone* for truth.

And this is the part *Attributes* and their Contradictories play in our knowledge of Reality. Attributes are the lights, and Contradictories the shades, which together work out some magnificent truth of Being; just as an artist represents the idea, Tree, on paper, by means of- black dots, and lines, — and light spaces. The idea, tree, is made manifest by means of the LAW OF CONTRADICTORIES, and *cannot be done in any other way*. Why? Because the artist is imitating *Nature*, and in nature, the idea is worked out on the principle of Contradictories; for phenomena are but mental pictures for the ideas of Infinite Mind.

In like manner all the great truths of Health, Virtue and Life are worked out of this same principle of Contradictories; But mankind, at present, as it were, accept them only nominally, or on trial. There is but one way to establish them as grand Realities. When the appearances called Evil, Disease and Death, are seen to be results of personifying self-evident unthinkables; then Health, Virtue and Eternal Life will be as absolutely certain as the fact that all right-angles are equal.

If a man in looking at the drawing of the tree on paper, should see only a meaningless collection of black lines and dots, and should devote himself to a minute analysis and enumeration of dots, angles, and straggling and crooked lines, he might display a very profound erudition on the whole subject of lines and dots; but he would forever miss the *idea Tree* in the artist's mind.

If on the other hand, another man should devote himself to the study of the phenomena of *light spaces*, he might work out some very marvelous theories involving laws of Optics and Mathematics; but he would also forever miss the idea, Tree in the artist's mind.

But if, finally, some one should, in looking at the sketch, arrive instantaneously and unconsciously at the idea, *tree*, lights and shades would be quite meaningless, in themselves, and never interest him beyond the fact that they represent the principle by means of which the idea was expressed.

Like Socrates of old, he would claim no wisdom for himself, simply because he had recognized the design of the artist, but would feel more than ever impelled to affirm that he knew nothing, in view of the fact that he was neither the Author of the idea, nor the sketch, nor the principle by which it was executed. If the Oracle pronounced him the wisest of men, he would maintain that it was simply because he knew nothing, while the ERUDITES of the Dark Lines and Light Spaces did not even know they knew nothing.

So if the ego could, with the humility of a little child, or with the Wisdom of Socrates, starting out once more from the Threshold of Knowledge, arrive instantaneously and unconsciously at the sublime ideas of Life and Love, contradictories would be quite meaningless in themselves and never more be of interest, save as they had together manifested the ideas of Life and Love and furnished the *Principle* whereby other ideas of INFINITE MIND could be comprehended by the *Finite*.

Cyrus Augustus Bartol

Teacher

Personified Unthinkables, published in Detroit in 1884, reflects the influence of Cyrus Bartol and his doctrine of mental pictures. Sarah's marriage to Archibald Grimké had brought her into the orbit of his Hyde Park relatives, who like Bartol were Unitarians with a sympathetic interest in Christian Science. Another Hyde Park resident adopted mental pictures as a key element in her own belief system. *First Lessons in Reality*, published two years later, reflects the influence of Mrs. Elizabeth Stuart, who had treated Sarah for heart disease and attributed her organic illness to her despairing husband. The dissolution of her marriage had begun when *Personified Unthinkables* was published and was complete by the time *First Lessons in Reality* appeared. Stuart was part of a group resignation from the Christian Scientist Association in 1881, and had formed an independent New Thought organization, named Light, Love, Truth, in the interval between Sarah's two publications. J.F. Eby, Printer, of Detroit was the publisher of each, implying that these first two sections were self-published. Only in the final portion of *Esoteric Lessons*, *A Tour Through the Zodiac*, do we find evidence of association with the Hermetic Brotherhood of Luxor, whose leaders published the collection after Sarah's death.

The entire record of Elizabeth's Stuart's affiliation with Mary Baker Eddy is dated in a single year. In her first letter dated January 25, 1881, Stuart referred to Eddy's "visit to us and your words of encouragement" and expressed her "earnest desire to heal the sick through the Understanding of Truth" which had already "met with a good share of success" despite the fact that she had been unsuccessful in becoming "free from some old Beliefs." This was as a result of having had surgery for removal of a fibroid tumor the previous winter, which had left her with residual symptoms that made her fear a recurrence. She asked Eddy for "seven or ten treatments or Lessons, for the unfolding of my spiritual perceptions" and asked the cost.[50]

Two months later, Stuart wrote again following a meeting of the Christian Scientist Association that Eddy had been unable to attend. She alluded to a suggestion by Eddy that Edward Arens was trying to deter her from embracing Christian Science, writing that "I am not easily moved from a firm determination, and I have not the slightest fear of Dr. Arens if my weapons are not stronger than his, then let me go down...we will return Good for Evil and thus disarm all enemies."[51] She closed with an expression of desire to take class instruction from Eddy, writing "I will wait with patience the summons to the feast."[52] In April, she and Jane L. Straw addressed a formal joint request to Eddy: "Having become mystified, by one Edward Arens, with regard to the Science of Healing, we now come to you, to learn that which, we believe, him incapable of Teaching, namely, Metaphysics."[53] Stuart's next, undated, letter was entirely focused on Eddy's struggles with Arens over his plagiarism of *Science and Health*. She advised Eddy to let the matter "die a natural death," arguing that "it is too <u>low</u> for your name to be associated with him in the Courts....work <u>silently</u> and we will work with you: vanquish him that way."[54] Stuart and Jane Straw issued an undated statement repudiating Arens: "We studied Mrs Eddy's system of metaphysical healing of Edward J Arens but he did not teach it and we did not understand it as we have since learned. And we did not learn of him how to heal the sick according to metaphysics."[55] In June Stuart and Straw were among 22 signers of an affidavit defending Eddy against criticisms from her former students: The signers testified "that we have studied Mary M.B. Eddy's system of metaphysics" and "know her to be a highly conscientious pure minded Christian woman.[56] The same week, Stuart and others personally appeared before a Justice of the Peace in Essex County, and swore under oath to the truth of the affidavit."[57]

Although Eddy chose not to prosecute Arens for plagiarism, she did denounce him in a revised third edition of *Science and Health*, which Stuart had advised against doing.[58] In a third, undated letter, Stuart addressed Eddy as "My Darling," and explained that her wish to visit her in Lynn had been thwarted by her own health problems. On Monday October 15, she reported being better, able to go into the city by train to visit her own patients, and confident that "the dawn is breaking the clouds are tipped with roseate hues, and soon very soon our horizon will be cloudless. Their poisoned arrows can no more penetrate the armour of Truth than the worm which crawls at your feet can pluck the Stars from the firmament. Each arrow rebounds with double force upon its owner."[59] Although Stuart had reported to the other students that Arens would "order his students to 'take up' Mrs. Eddy mentally," she was disinclined to believe this had affected Eddy's health.[60] The last letter she wrote to Eddy was an undated note written later in October, which closed with assurance of support in the struggle with Arens, but her methods apparently were so repellent that Eddy never replied: "Mrs. S. – and - myself will fasten our fangs into them and Compel them to Stop, I will not leave you night nor day, but will employ my Thoughts like hot Shells unto their camp. God will help the Right and vanquish the foe."[61]

The group resignation from the Christian Scientist Association was dated October 21, only six days later. Stuart and seven others signed a proclamation to the effect that Eddy's "frequent ebullitions of temper, love of money, and the appearance of hypocrisy" left them no choice but to "most respectfully withdraw our names from the Christian Science Association and Church of Christ (Scientist)."[62] Five days later on October 26, with Mrs. Eddy in the Chair, the CSA met at her home and unanimously passed a vote to the effect that "your unchristian communication of Oct. 21, 81, renders you liable to Church disipline" and that "You are hereby notified to appear before the Church of Christ (Scintist) at 8 Broad St. Lynn on Monday Oct 31 At 5 P.M. To answer for unjust proceeding."[63] None of the dissidents attended, but ten days later the remaining members voted to expel Howard, Rice, and Rawson for "conduct unbecoming a Christian Scientist." Stuart was expelled for "unconstitutional conduct" and there was some reference to "arsenical poisoning" in the proceedings.

On November 2, Eddy wrote to William Stuart, objecting to his "highly improper language and false statements" to an unnamed male disciple which revealed how he was influenced "by the silent arguments of those lying in wait to fulfill their threats to ruin my reputation and stop my labors for the uplifting of the race." Eddy protested that she had refused to accept Mrs. Stuart as a patient but accepted her as a pupil after "ceaseless IMPORTUNITIES."[64] Less than week later, on November 8, Eddy wrote to Clara E. Choate blaming James E. Howard and Miranda Rice for swaying the other six to resign: "I have learned for a certainty that Howard and Mrs Rice carried the other five by making you the issue."[65] When Howard, Rice, and others were subsequently expelled on October 31 for "conduct unbecoming a Christian Scientist"[66] Stuart was expelled on the lesser charge of "unconstitutional conduct," yet she was singled out for more criticism in subsequent years than any of the others who resigned simultaneously.

The harshest criticism was made in an article that in its final version concealed the name of Elizabeth Stuart and the author of the piece. Edmund G. Hardy's "Workings of Animal Magnetism," published in August 1889 in the *Christian Science Journal*, was published after extensive editing by Calvin Frye. The proofs of Hardy's original text survive in the Mary Baker Eddy Library and are far more revealing than the final product. Hardy had given a report of his acquaintance with Stuart and Eddy to a recent class instruction and was requested to repeat the information for the Journal. He wrote:

> Six years ago I went for healing to Mrs. William Stuart, then claiming to heal by Christian Science in Hyde Park, Mass. After receiving relief, and as I then believed healing, I sought to know the process by which she was enabled to do this work...This search led me to "SCIENCE AND HEALTH," and then to Mrs. Eddy. Mrs. Eddy very kindly gave me nearly an entire evening, during which I related my experience. She spoke no word denouncing Mrs. Stuart, but did call to my attention the false and the true teaching, and said to me, "I

hope, Mr. Hardy, that when you study you will get the truth." I returned to Mrs. Stuart, joyful in the thought that I had met Mrs. Eddy, but imagine the confusion of mind when I was met by the one whom I believed to have healed me, with the declaration that Mrs. Eddy had departed from the path of Science, into selfishness, mesmerism, &c., and assured me that she had used this power on the very night of my call to make her sick; that she never was so sick in her life as at the very time I was in conversation with Mrs. Eddy.[67]

Hardy reveals Stuart in 1883 as intensely antagonistic and competitive towards Eddy, making accusations of mesmerism, just as she was gaining an unhealthy influence over Sarah, according to her husband and his family.

Theodore Weld had been present with his fellow Hyde Park Unitarian William Stuart at a May 25, 1881 meeting of the Christian Scientist Association, where they both were listed as "visiting friends" who participated in remarks about the "good of the order."[68] William Stuart was a pall bearer for Theodore Weld in 1895, but for much of the intervening period there was tension between the families. Although Weld was an early Mind Cure enthusiast, his only letter to Mrs. Eddy was a denunciation of gossip in which she had engaged with an unidentified "Mrs. S.," probably Elizabeth Stuart. He wrote on November 21, 1881, complaining that his niece Mrs. Day had heard reports of gossip that she was regarded as a "a perfect disgrace to the family" who "dressed herself as she did in order to attract the notice of gentlemen" and that the family "wished she would go back where she came from." Weld indignantly denied all these charges, writing "To all of this I have only to say-that none of us ever had the least suspicion that Mrs. Day had in her styles...gait in walking & independent manner, expression of countenance, erect attitude & dignified...presence which distinguishes her the least thought of thereby attracting the notice of gentlemen or any others. That air manners &c were born with her & it is a personal idiosyncracy & nothing else. As to a disgraceful family history connected with her none of us ever heard or suspected the existence of any such thing...ever said that she was a disgrace to us-- never thought ...never known or heard that some one questioned her moral character in the least particular. She has always moved in the most respectable circles of society & has always been well regarded & spoken of ...entitled to distinguished consideration."[69]

Archibald Henry Grimké

Sarah's involvement with Elizabeth Stuart would lead to the end of her marriage. At the time of her separation from Archibald, the response of Moses Stanley shows that he was no racist opponent of the marriage, but earnestly hoped to save it. In May 1883 Archie wrote to his father in law after Sarah had announced that she did not intend to return to Boston from a vacation she had taken with their daughter Angelina to Michigan:

She seemed unhappy – she was unwell. I believed that much of her ill health was caused by the inactive & apathetic life she was living – but still I think we might have got from under the cloud but for the happening of one of the most important events in our marriage life. It was Sarah's treatment by Mrs. Stuart. You know about Mrs. Stuart? Well her theory is that every disease is produced by some fear. Each patient she treats she endeavors to discover the cause of the disease. It is no matter what cause she has fastened on as the pregnant one—if she could make Sarah believe it—it of course will produce some effect proportioned to the current of the belief of the patient. She found the cause and occasion of Sarah's ailments to be grounded in her relations to me. What Sarah lacked was something positive—some active principle—Mrs. Stuart declared that Sarah's relations to me had destroyed her will—her individuality—had reduced her to a state of mental and moral subjection. She held me up before Sarah in the character of an oppressor—a selfish & lordly man—mark you however this woman had never seen us together but once & knew nothing of us except what Sarah had told her & what she had added too by the aid of her imagination.... I felt that to be called an oppressor when I had not scrupled to do all the house work—such as washing dishes—emptying chamber pots—sweeping rooms—making beds—taking in the clothes—in short doing without a murmur every thing which women ordinarily were accustomed to do-- & all to save my wife—yes sir to be called an oppressor & the author of my wife's diseases—seemed more than I could or ought to bear. I called Sarah's attention to the fact that she had been sick before she knew me at all—that Dr. Sofford [*Daniel Spofford—ed*] who treated her when a student in Boston University had told me that she was diseased + naturally delicate—that before she left home at all her life had been despaired of by her own statement the Drs. At Ann Arbor had pronounced her disease of the heart organic...[70]

Moses replied on May 22, 1883, from Mackinac Island, "You are both dear to me and I earnestly wish & desire to do what shall be for your mutual good. I think you are correct as to the cause of all—poor health & the most extremely sensitive organization. She has never been well since she had the scarlet fever in her 4th year. She went to Boston an invalid, & it is ungenerous as it is unjust, for Mrs. Stuart or Sarah or anyone to charge you with her poor health so please stick that arrow in the fire & never let it prick you again. You are conscious of having done what you could to make her happy--let that comfort you."[71]

Archibald Grimké and his old friend and mentor Frances Pillsbury shared an equally negative view of Mrs. Stuart. Pillsbury had been headmaster of the Charleston school in which Archibald and his brothers were enrolled at the end of the Civil War, and was instrumental in arranging for them to study at Lincoln University in Pennsylvania. Her husband Gilbert, brother of famed abolitionist Parker Pillsbury, had been the Reconstruction mayor of Charleston for several years. They returned to Massachusetts before Archie went there to study. In an 1873 letter written soon after his arrival at Harvard, Frances exulted in his good fortune to be embraced by his Grimké aunts and Theodore Weld, and recalled the last time she had seen him, sailing away from South Carolina:

> Ah! Archie, when I think of you a halo of light and happiness seems to surround you, & a great happiness lightens my thoughts. That you are really at Cambridge drinking from the very fountain you desire, that you are so perfect yourself, winning love & respect from all—that you are beloved & cared for by the noblest and tenderest of families your uncle and aunt Weld is more than a satisfaction...Thank heaven for the flowery harbor into which the storms have driven you!"[72]

Frances Pillsbury became Archie's closest confidante after Sarah left, judging from his extant correspondence, and she shared his sense of outrage at the role of Elizabeth Stuart in inciting Sarah to end the marriage. The flowery harbor of life in Boston was to become stormy, and Archie blamed the Welds' friends and neighbors the Stuarts more than he blamed Sarah. In an undated letter from 1883, Archie wrote to Moses Stanley blaming Elizabeth Stuart not just for instigating Sarah's original departure, but also for undermining Stanley's attempt to reconcile them. "I wrote Sarah in the terrible agony of my grief to have mercy on me- I prayed her forgiveness- I besought her save me with her love- the appeal touched her her love & tenderness & loyalty reasserted themselves for a moment—Mrs. Stuart hearing that Sarah was irresolute whether to go or return wrote her a pack of falsehoods—about what I had said to my uncle about her. And this the second opportunity slipped by me & was lost."[73]

In his first letter to Sarah after she announced that she would not return from Michigan, Archie made very clear that he considered the Stuarts to blame:

> You are in no condition at present to view this matter dispassionately & fairly. You can only see your side – & your side as it has appeared to your friend Mrs. Stuart. I do verily believe that you are entirely under her control, & cannot think your own thoughts or do your own will if she interferes...Well then dear the morning that you intended to leave- you will remember that I asked you whether you intended to return & I then said that if you stayed in Mass. I would take Nana away from you- & Mrs. S? I had an indefinite apprehension that you & others were plotting against me- that your action for two months or six weeks was the result of some secret understanding between you & others, I felt that the Stuarts were in this – that morning when I said I would take Nana away from you it was because I somehow felt that you might go to live with the Stuarts & take Nana there & defy me to take her or to have any thing to do with her. [74]

Evidently Sarah had complained that Archie had induced the Welds to consider her insane, and Stuart had been the bearer of this message, as he continued:

> Do not say that I have destroyed or shaken the trust of the Welds in your word or sanity—For Uncle Theodore discovered the above discrepancy between the statement which you made to Mrs. Stuart & the one which you afterwards made to him - & this my dear he volunteered to tell me. And as to the matter of your sanity- he said that he discovered something in your countenance which suggested possibilities in the direction of insanity long before he ever spoke to me about you.[75]

Frances Pillsbury began to serve as a go-between, or informant, as soon as the bad news arrived. On May 24, she wrote to Archie that she had received a letter from Sarah in Ann Arbor, in which "She said in the letter that I should be <u>surprised</u> to hear from her out West and also should be **shocked** if you "had written me any particulars," as he obviously had done.[76] On June 27 she followed up with a report that she had written Sarah as Archie had desired: "Have written six pages—all about the farm & flowers & carriage house. I told her the carriage was newly painted and covered to be ready to carry Nana & Sarah to ride when they returned! I said not a syllable that would show that I knew anything about affairs."[77] Her next letter, written October 8, blames Moses Stanley for harboring Sarah rather than sending her home to Archie: "For it is in his power to send your wife & child back to you, if he chooses—Sarah would never stay away in this manner if her relatives showed her the <u>wrong of it</u>. Now Archie I have thought of one way to open the Reverend clergyman's eyes. This is to write him an anonymous letter giving him an account of Mrs. Stewart's witchcraft- of her ascribing demonic powers & acts to you – of her outrageous money making & promising patients to nine other weak women in the same village &c &c—I think that kind of ointment for Mr. Stanley's eyes—would be equal to the clay that Jesus used in the blind man—it would cause him to SEE."[78] It is unclear whether or not she did so, but in November she reported having gotten another letter from Sarah. The reply in question was enclosed and was a terse communication that opened a period of great stress over Angelina's custody. "Thanks for your kind letter, enclosing one from Archie. In reply I have only to say that I do not intend to ever return to live with Archie....P/S/ I should be glad to know explicitly Archie's wishes, or intentions in regard to the child, since she is legally his. S.S.G."[79] Although there is no known connection between Gilbert and Frances Pillsbury and Christian Science, Parker was later to write very cordially to Eddy, whose sister had married a Pillsbury cousin in New Hampshire decades earlier.[80] An April 3, 1891 letter from Eddy to Laura E. Sargent ends with a PS asking "How do you like Parker Pillsbury's pamphlet? [81] A note in the files of J.C. Tomlinson's 1907 reminiscences indicates some pride in the association with "the well known Pillsbury family the members of which have attained wide celebrity in business and in Reform movements."[82]

Sarah sent Archie a mixed message about Angelina's support on September 22, 1884, writing "I wish to be assured that you fully relinquish your claim to her person, and freely entrust her care and education in my hands. And, further, I wish to know whether in so doing you would still consider it a pleasure as well as a duty to assist in her maintenance."[83] She also asked Archie how much he would be willing and able to contribute monthly or annually. His reply was dated September 26, and he assured her "that I consider your claim to Nana's person higher than my own, that your wishes and interests in regard to her person and education to take precedence over mine in all respects when yours and mine are in non agreement" and also "that had I the moral right to decide as to her custody & education I know of no one to whom I would more fully & freely commit the dear little girl than to your mother love & dutiful care." While considering it a duty and pleasure to provide financial support, he was unclear about Sarah's remark about relinquishing his claims, asking if "in case of your death before me, I am not then to claim my child?" and concluding by asking for a suggested amount needed for Angelina's support.

Although his investments had failed and his income was meagre, he saw prospects for financial improvement in the "public position & reputation" he had recently attained. In a postscript he reminded Sarah of a life insurance policy of two thousand dollars which would be due to her in the event of his death.[84] Four days later she wrote a reply, thanking him for his letter and the enclosed check and proposing two hundred dollars per year as a fair amount for child support. She assured him that "in case of my death before yours, no one will dispute your claim to your child. I only wish to be equally certain that I am not liable to have her taken from me at any moment- even if I should so so unlikely a thing as to visit Massachusetts again."[85]

This arrangement was only to last three months, as on January 11, 1885 Sarah changed her mind and wrote to Archie that she had "come to realize that it is not for the best good & happiness of our little girl to be brought up under divided claims. As matters now stand, she is legally yours, and while you support her, you have claims, and also, she is yours in case of my death. But she ought to be either wholly yours or wholly mine. I therefore wish to assume, at once, her entire support & education, & in case of my death I wish her left free to choose between you & my people." Thanking him for his past services, she concluded with an ominous remark that seems directed at his friendship with the Pillsburys: "And allow me, now, to most solemnly warn you that the one you call your good fairy is your evil genius, in that she prompts you to seek fame & power instead of Peace & Good-will. The Earthly, instead of the Celestial."[86] On January 18 he replied that he was greatly surprised by her change of heart, having considered the recent agreement a final conclusion to discussion of competing claims. While he could not understand what motivated this sudden decision, he felt that he "must trust that you understand fully what you wish & that it is indeed for the best good & happiness of our little girl" but left the door open to further reconsideration on her part. Sarah's change of heart seems to have coincided with a change in Elizabeth Stuart's status, as she had decided to create her own independent Mind Cure group which would use Sarah's lessons as part of its curriculum. In

December 1884, Sarah H. Crosse wrote a letter to the *Christian Science Journal* addressed "To Whom it May Concern" warning that "An aggressive outside element of which the public should be informed is this: Many are assuming the name `Christian Scientist' who never belonged to the Christian Scientist Association; some even who have been expelled from it. This mixes things. Long before the people in Hyde Park heard of metaphysical healing, or Mrs. Elizabeth Stuart was taught it by Mrs. Eddy in 1881, the name was given by Mrs. Eddy to this organization, and *none but its members have any right to it.*"[87] This implies that Stuart was seen by Christian Scientists as an unscrupulous usurper, but she seems to have abandoned use of the term "Christian Science" the following year.

In May 1885 Elizabeth Stuart taught a class in Hartford, Connecticut, which was followed in December by her student Leander Edmund Whipple becoming a mental healer there. This ultimately led to Hartford becoming the center for her group's work, which had already been organized in Massachusetts and New York under the name "Light, Love, Truth." The triangular symbol adopted by the group was interpreted to mean "Life cannot be manifested apart from Love and Truth. Love cannot be separated from Life and Truth. Without Truth there can be neither Life nor Love."[88] In August 1885, Sarah announced a correspondence class entitled "First Lessons in Reality, OR The Psychical Basis of Physical Health." Pupils were directed to write to her at 31 Milwaukee Avenue, Detroit, her parents' address. The method of instruction was explained:

> Each member will receive a list of questions, together with a copy of the lesson to be studied. Answers are to be prepared by the student and forwarded for correction, explanation, etc., after which the MS. Of the student will be returned, and a second lesson and list of questions received for study.

The course consisted of thirteen lessons, with a tuition fee of $10.00, "students paying their own postage."[89]

At the beginning of 1886, Archie made one final effort to reconcile with Sarah, writing to her that "after two persons are married they should, where it is at all possible, endeavor to live together" and in light of Angelina's welfare, "I therefore Sarah earnestly write you to return home so that together we may take up life's duties until death do us part" which he signed "your husband."[90] Her reply does not survive and perhaps never was made directly, but that summer she wrote to their former landlady in Hyde Park, Mrs. Leverett. This letter apparently expressed another change of heart about Angelina in light of Archie's next letter to her, dated July 12. He wrote: "Mrs. Leverett showed me your letter on Saturday morning in answer I desire to say to you that I would be very happy to take our dear little Nana & devote my life to her—You might then remain where you now are or if otherwise inclined return with the dear little one to the home which has had its door open to receive you every day & hour since you left it more than three years ago. My means do not allow me to discharge my duties to Nana by any other arrangement. Tell Nana that her dear Papa wants very much to see her tho."[91]

During the first years of the group Light, Love, Truth, Sarah appears to have been the sole published author of lessons. Neither Mrs. Stuart nor her close colleague Emma Austin Tolles of Hartford became published authors, but the Grimké correspondence affords several clues to her role as amanuensis for their group. Most of her letters to Angelina from the period are undated and lack return addresses, but internal evidence shows their sequence. References to Elizabeth Stuart and Emma Tolles are abundant. In summer 1887 Sarah wrote to Angelina, "My dear little Girl; Your good letters have reached me safely with Mrs. Tolles letters" asking later "Have you been away any where with Mrs. Stuart."[92] Angelina was evidently in the company of both Tolles and Stuart during her years at school in Hyde Park, where the Weld family had apparently reconciled with the Stuarts. Sarah's initial move to California might have been influenced by the presence in San Francisco of Miranda R. Rice, a former colleague of Mrs. Eddy who had seceded from Christian Science ranks the same day as her sister Dorcas Rawson and Elizabeth Stuart. Sarah did not remain in the Bay Area; although *First Lessons in Reality* was published in Detroit, its foreword was signed Los Angeles, California, June 1886. Weeks earlier, on April 3, Sarah had signed her pledge in Los Angeles as a member of the Hermetic Brotherhood of Luxor. While in California, Sarah wrote to her daughter indicating that her friend Mrs. Rice had seen Angelina at Mrs. Stuart's: "I have just had a letter from Mrs. Rice and she tells me she saw you one day at Mrs. Stuarts."[93] Emma Austin Tolles evidently was concerned that Angelina have proper clothing, as shown by another 1887 letter from Sarah: "If you like the things Mrs. Tolles sent I wish you would write and thank her. She tells me she has some new shoes for you and some other things almost ready to send – you know her address –"[94] following up in her next letter:

> I most sincerely hope that you can go and see Mrs. Tolles some time in Hartford. She has been a very good friend to you in the past, and will be in the future. You can depend on it...Your good letter made mamma very happy. I want you to improve in your writing as fast as you can, so as to write lessons and books when you get older, just as mamma does. Then, you know, you can go to California, or Detroit, or any where in the world you wish. I am glad the things from Mrs. Tolles reached you all right. Has she sent you shoes yet? I am glad you have such jolly times at Mrs. Stuart's, with Mr. Stuart, and with Maggie...Mamma is very much better now, and has already gone to writing on the lessons again and hopes to finish them this time. I hope my little girl is both good and happy in Hyde Park.[95]

James Henry Wiggin always gave frank advice to Eddy in his role as editor, after giving up the Unitarian ministry which he had long practiced in the Boston area. He explained to her "If I see a rock ahead in a friend's track, in one sense it is none of my business which way his craft takes; yet in another sense I feel constrained to speak: and that answering her critics would be beneath her dignity and that of the Journal." Wiggin was editor of the *Christian Science*

Journal from 1886 until 1889 and worked intermittently as an editor for Mrs. Eddy in the 1890s. He offered advice similar to that provided some years earlier by William Stuart, but perhaps older and wiser in the wake of negative publicity by 1888, she took his advice to heart when he cautioned against engaging in controversy with her enemies. For example, on July 1, 1888 he commented about two such proposed articles "Don't allow yourself to be led into the printing of these articles. Yr cause can not afford it – There is trouble enough in yr camp, & unwisdom shd not be allowed to aggravate it. Such documents will make outsiders laugh, while yr judicious friends grieve."[96] The *Journal* did however repudiate both Stuart and Grimké in 1887.

A debunking 1887 article in the *Century* entitled "Christian Science and Mind Cure" described the teachings of Stuart and Grimké as well as those of Edward Arens. The author James Monroe Buckley quoted Stuart making extreme claims for her mental treatments, for example "A woman came to me who had suffered five years with what the doctors called rheumatism. I happened to know that the death of a child had caused this effect. By silently erasing that picture of death and holding in its place an image of Life, eternal Life, she was entirely cured in twenty minutes."[97] In another quoted passage Buckley extends his ridicule of Stuart to her experiments with mental treatment of animals, a case of mange in a dog named Carlo.[98] In August 1887, the *Christian Science Journal* (under Wiggin's editorship) felt compelled to dissociate itself from both Stuart and Grimké in the wake of the critical article in the *Century* that used the term Christian Scientist to refer to various dissidents. It noted that "Mrs. Stuart studied at Metaphysical College, but also with Mr. Arens, and no longer affiliates with the College Association; and Miss Grimké was never in the Founder's classes."[99]

The only other reference to Sarah in the Journal had appeared in a letter from "M.W." of Columbus, Wisconsin in the January 1885 issue. The writer dismissed an unnamed work by "S.S. Grimké," which would be *Personified Unthinkables*, along with two other recent Mind Cure publications in which there is "nothing added to your first words which cover all the ground."[100] This contrasts sharply with elaborate praise directed at Sarah Moore Grimké and her sister Angelina, as well as the still-living Theodore Weld, in the April 1886 issue. An unsigned article "Two Noble Sisters," presumably written by Wiggin who had recently become editor, extolled them in the highest terms from the perspective of a personal acquaintance.

Eddy seems to have been deeply disappointed by Miranda Rice's defection. In October 1877 she had a vision of John the Revelator, in which "To Miranda he said, pointing her to me, "here is your first duty, to help her, to support her, and for this you have been set apart."[101] Three years after her defection, Eddy forwarded some correspondence to Rice, adding a note which said "I whom you have so DEEPLY wronged can forgive you and rejoice in any good you may do for the cause for which I have laid down all of earth that you and others might gain heaven."[102] Forgiveness does not seem to have been Eddy's attitude toward Elizabeth Stuart. The only instance of Eddy relating Stuart to themes in her classes is found in Joshua Bailey's notes of her Primary Class of March 1889. It consists of disconnected fragments that are hard to decipher, but the gist is that Stuart's "cancer" had been caused by mental malpractice and that she "shut her heart against Mrs. Eddy." She went on to discuss a case of Stuart having gotten a cinder in her eye, which was instantly cured in class when Mrs. Eddy spoke, but thereafter Stuart herself took credit for the healing. Somehow Cyrus Bartol was connected to this incident, and discussed it with Eddy, who told the class that a recent article in the Journal "showed reason of hating Mrs. Stewart, about rabbit, cats, birds...would take children next."[103] As extreme as this language seems, Archibald Grimké and his old friend and mentor Frances Pillsbury shared an equally negative view of Mrs. Stuart.

There is no return address on the April 25, 1887 letter in which Sarah announces to Archie that she is returning Angelina to him after four years of sole custody, on grounds of race. Another letter in the Moorland-Spingarn archives suggests that Sarah was in Kansas with Angelina that spring. Angelina received a letter from her former teacher Frances Morehead dated June 26, 1887: "I think you were a brave girl to take such a long trip alone. Did no one have the care of you all the way from Kansas to Boston?"[104] Sarah wrote:

> Within the past few weeks I have been obliged to suspend all work and I now realize that it is for the best good and happiness of little Nana that she should go to you at once. She is so very happy at the prospect of going to see her papa that – I am quite reconciled to resign her to you (at least for the present). She is really much more like you than myself and you can control her better than I have been able to do. In many ways I have been too strict – in others, not strict enough. But just now I am both physically and mentally unfit to have the care of her at all. She needs that love and sympathy of one of her own race which I am sure her father still has for her; but which it is impossible for others to give... I am in hopes to resume my work of teaching in the Fall and may visit Hartford, Ct. during the season still I leave the future to take care of itself, only trying to do the very best possible for the present.[105]

The only dated letter from this period was written July 15, 1887. Sarah wrote that she was very happy to learn of the Fourth of July celebrations in Hartford where Angelina had been with Mrs. Tolles and friends, "A new doll, - a new dress and a glorious Fourth of July with fire crackers and torpedos etc. etc. makes me feel, too, as though I were having a good time with you in Hartford. I know of No place which has such a hold upon me as Hartford. I expect I shall come there some time, but not yet. I do not know when. It may be a long time. There is some hard work for me to do first."[106]

Stuart proclaimed the mission of her new group on the final day of a historic conference that included Elizabeth Cady Stanton, Susan B. Anthony, and Frederick Douglass. Her address was given April 1, 1888 at the International Council of Women convened in

Boston by the National Woman Suffrage Association, under the title "The Power of Thought":

> The imaging faculty is the highest known to man; through it he expresses the ideal, and it is the means by which he expresses to the senses whatever intellect accepts, thus forming the relation between mind and body. Through that open door fear enters and stamps upon the body distorted, untrue mental images, which physicians name, then proceed to try to erase from the body....[107]

It does not appear that Sarah was able to return to Hartford, and just over a year later she announced her intention to leave the United States. On May 11, 1888 she wrote to Archie asking for a divorce, and informing him that she intended on reverting to her maiden name:

> Our marriage relationship exists only in name, and can never be otherwise. These thoughts have recently assumed more definite shape owing to my having received very favorable offers of literary work abroad... In preparing to leave the U.S. I wish to reassume my maiden name, also to have this whole matter settled once and forever, and as promptly as possible...Should you refuse to grant so just a settlement of the inharmony existing between us, I can only say, that it will make no difference to my plans. I shall leave the U.S., and reassume my own name, just the same. Still I would prefer to have our separation made legal, so as to be on friendly terms with you, and to remain in communication with Nana.[108]

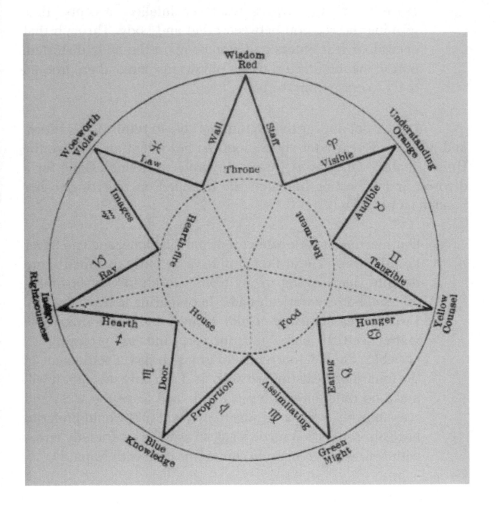

FIRST LESSONS IN REALITY

OR THE PSYCHICAL BASIS

OF PHYSICAL HEALTH

PREFACE.

The following lessons are now given to the public without the slightest alteration, just as they were prepared, and taught by correspondence to a few friends and fellow seekers after *Truth*.

Although it would seem desirable, because of their somewhat mystical nature, to attempt to fortify them against misconception, yet experience has taught that the attempt would, after all, but court the very danger to be avoided.

To interpret them *too literally* will be to lose their essence. On the other hand, not to discern the vital relations between the ideas herein expressed, and the *symbols embodying* them, will be equally fatal to their true apprehension; for the terms employed are not as one might suppose merely fanciful, figurative, poetic, etc., but are used because they express the dual unity of *Thought* and *Symbol*.

To have a knowledge of facts is one thing, but to grasp the relation of these facts to each other, is quite another thing. One mind can help another in the former case, but in the latter each soul must discern relations for itself. This discerning must be *inborn*, it cannot be imparted. One *cannot* discern a relation for another any more than a joke can be appreciated vicariously. So in these lessons *Thought* and *Symbol* have been placed in juxtaposition, the insight into their relation must be left to the Soul in travail with *Truth*.

Los Angeles, California, July, 1886

SYNOPSIS

Introduction — The Staff.

1. REFLECTION.

	(Visible.		(Hunger.
Ray-ment	(Audible.	Food	(Eating.
	(Tangible.		(Assimilating.

2. REFRACTION.

	(Proportion.		(Ray.
House	(Door.	Hearth-fire	(Images.
	(Hearth.		(Law.

CONCLUSION— THE WALL

FIRST LESSONS IN REALITY

INTRODUCTION.

THE STAFF.

One end of a staff implies another end. I cannot (as tradition relates of a certain Hibernian philosopher) cut off one end from my staff, and then have only one end left. I may thus reduce the size of my staff, but while it holds out it continues to have two ends. Neither do the two ends remain after the staff has gone. The staff and its ends are real, or polar opposites, which mutually imply each other, which are utterly meaningless and unthinkable apart.

However, although I cannot detach the staff from its ends, nor the ends from the staff, yet I can distinguish between them. One end is not the other end. The head is not the foot of the staff, neither is the foot the head. There must, therefore, be some invisible point of union between the two. A point which is neither the one end nor the other, but where the two are one. This invisible centre I take to be the point of equilibrium. I, therefore, balance my staff until I find this point. Now but one thing remains to make my staff *living*, to turn the *rod* into a *serpent*, and that is *motion*. The motion of my staff about its invisible centre is circular, a form of *spiral*. Spiral is from the Latin spira, meaning *breath*, coil, spire, etc. *Spirit* is from the same word. Motion is, accordingly, the breath of life.

The staff as a whole expresses *Unity*; as composed of polar opposites it is a *Duality*; as polar opposites and point of equilibrium, a Trinity; as living it manifests a *Quarterni*, — the sacred Quarterni of Pythagoras.

The two ends of the staff, as visible, symbolize the phenomenal, or terrestrial portions of this Quarterni. Point of equilibrium, and motion, as invisible, symbolize the more *real* and celestial elements.

Having learned this much of the nature of the rod, I wish to know what use I am to make of it in the study of Reality. Finding that the words *real, ray, thing* and *thought* are all derived from the word meaning *Rod*, I conclude that Reality is Rod-ality, and that to spare the rod, in this study of Reality, would be to spoil the child.

Accordingly, my staff, whether I take it as a rod of light, or as a type of all vegetation, from the blade of grass to the tallest tree, symbolizes to me an invisible and more *real* rod of thing and *Ray of Thought*.

LESSON II.

RAY-MENT— VISIBLE.

 If, when standing beside a body of water, I chance to see the form of a cloud mirrored in golden and rosy tints upon its surface, I am not deceived by the picture. Beautiful as it is, I know that it is but a reflection of a cloud in the sky, far above my head, which I do not see as long as my attention is directed to the cloud upon the water. I know that, although I thus distinguish between the cloud upon the water and the cloud in the sky, I cannot *separate* the one from the other. I cannot *detach* the cloud upon the water from the one in the sky, and still have my picture upon the water after the picture in the sky has drifted away beyond the horizon.

Still further, I know that as my cloud upon the water depends upon the cloud in the sky, so they both depend upon the light from the sun, and that while my picture upon the water is simply a *reflection* produced by the action of rays of light and the reaction of the surface of the water, so the picture in the sky is a *refraction* produced by the action of rays of light and a reaction of vapor in the atmosphere. My cloud celestial, and my cloud terrestrial, are each a *Ray-ment* (rod-ment) resulting from an action and a reaction.

But if I cannot separate the refracted picture from the reflected picture, then there must be some invisible point of union between the two, a centre of equilibrium between the action implied in the term *refraction*, and the reaction implied in the term *reflection*, a point which is neither celestial or terrestrial, but where the two are *One*.[109]

Looking again upon the water I behold my face reflected upon its surface, and then call to mind the fact that my own face I have never seen; its reflected image is all that I ever have seen, or can see. Now the reflected face upon the water is certainly only a ray-ment produced by the action of rays of light and the reaction of the surface of the water, and if, what I have hitherto considered my real face is only a rayment produced by an action and a reaction, the fact that it has never occurred to me proves nothing against its truth, especially when I remember that since *real* and *ray* are the same in derivation, from the meaning of the words, my real face is my ray face.

Turning my attention to my body, I conclude that if my face is ray-ment my whole body is ray-ment, produced by an invisible action and reaction. If, then, this terrestrial body or ray-ment is like my cloud terrestrial, simply an inverted reflect of my celestial ray-ment, the fact that I have never *consciously* recognized my celestial ray-ment proves nothing against its existence, for while my attention was directed exclusively to my cloud floating upon the water, I became for the time being entirely oblivious of the cloud above my head which I could not see.

But if this terrestrial ray-ment is only an inverted reflect of a true and celestial ray-ment, then I am possessor of an heritage hitherto unknown; for, like the two clouds, they cannot be *separated*, they are real (ray) or polar opposites which mutually imply each other, which are utterly meaningless and impossible apart. Now if my *consciousness* has been located, hitherto, solely within the reflected image of my true self, then I am a slave bound clown, by my own ignorance, to chains of sense and suffering. But with this recognition of my serfdom I also see clearly the way of escape.[110] There must be an invisible point of union between the two, and I must locate my consciousness at that invisible centre of equilibrium between my refracted and my reflected self, the point which is neither celestial nor terrestrial, but where the two are *One*.

The question of *how* to emancipate my consciousness from its inverted reflection and to locate it at its true and invisible centre, is the most momentous in the universe. It involves the meaning and object of existence. It is the problem of all times, that of the perfectibility and immortality of the *soul*. Of the *soul*, for this earthly *consciousness* is but the inverted reflection of my *true consciousness*, which is the same thing as soul. These first lessons in Reality, then, are first steps in the path of Rodality, — a straight and narrow ray of light!

Turning, therefore, to my staff, I state the problem in terms of rod. The two visible ends are terrestrial ray-ments; the head of the staff is the body; the foot of the staff is the purely finite or earthly mind; the point of equilibrium, or the invisible centre, where body and sensations are one, is consciousness; motion, the breath of life, completes this Quarterni.

Consciousness and motion symbolize the refracted or celestial elements of the Quarterni. Body and finite mind, the terrestrial portions. Body is the strictly visible member of this Quarterni. And body, again, as a whole, is four-fold, corresponding in structure to the four elements. The solids of the body (bones, tissues, etc.) correspond to earth. Heat, the agent of the functions especially connected with solids and between solids and liquids, correspond to the second element, or fire. Secretions of the body correspond to the third element, or water, while breath is the fourth element, or air.

The action of respiration and the reaction of secretions form an upper dualism, and to destroy, *e. g.*, the balance between the action of the lungs and the reaction of the blood, would instantly produce violent and even fatal results, from which the visible body would soon pass to the realm of the invisible.

The action of heat and the secretion of tissues form a lower dualism, and to destroy the balance between heat and tissues would likewise produce a wasting away of the visible body.

Now the harmonious equilibrium between these upper and lower dualisms is what is ordinarily termed physical health, and if, as I have already decided, equilibrium of body is simply a reflect of a celestial or soul equilibrium, then the basis of *physical health*, is purely *psychical*.

But as long as my consciousness is located within my body, body rules soul, whereas body hould be simply raiment (ray-ment) for my true consciousness.

Again, this raiment for my soul must be like all rays, or, like my staff. It must have two ends and a central point. I, therefore, regard the *Visible* as the head of my staff, the *Audible* as the foot, and the *Tangible* as the point which is neither visible nor audible, but where the two are one.

LESSON III.

RAY-MENT— AUDIBLE.

Once, by means of an aperture in a shutter, and a prism, I tried to detach a ray of sunlight from the sun, and shut it up within a dark room. It arranged itself in beautiful colors upon the wall, but when the sun went, the ray went too. So with each step in this study of Ray-ality I am confronted with the impossibility and unthinkability of any such thing as separateness. Thus, by means of refraction and reflection, combined according to definite numeral conditions, light becomes visible; also, by means of refraction and reflection combined according to definite numeral conditions, *breath becomes audible*; yet breath and light cannot be separated, for light without breath or *motion* would not be light, would not exist at all.

Still, although I cannot separate visible rays from audible rays, yet I must distinguish between them in order to reach an understanding of them. As a first step in distinguishing between visible and audible rays, I turn my attention to the *numeral conditions* according to which all external manifestation takes place. And in order to study numbers, I regard them as *visible numerals* and as *invisible numerals*.[111]

The visible numerals are three, viz., the point, and the two forms of the line, or, the straight line and the crooked line. When I draw a picture on a piece of paper, I use the three visible numerals. But in order to complete the manifestation, to make my picture living, there must be the light spaces of the paper to bring it out. A moment's reflection convinces me that the whole visible universe is pictured out to my vision solely by means of the three visible numerals in space. All the infinite variety is but gradation and combination of these primary numbers. The horizon gives me the perfect circle. The line from the zenith to my feet is the straight line. The outlines of the clouds present a loose combination of the straight and the crooked lines, while the rocks, trees, etc., of the earth's surface, display a more minute and compact combination of the two forms of line. Geometry, or the art of measuring the earth, as well as the whole science of Astronomy, depend upon these visible numerals, and with this thought comes to me the *meaning* of these visible numerals. The point symbolizes the centre of the two forms of line, or the point which is neither the straight line nor the crooked line, but where the two are one. Again, the straight line symbolizes the form of force which strikes out from the centre, termed in science the *centrifugal*; while the crooked line symbolizes the form of force which draws back to the centre, termed *centripetal*. Thus is all visible but the type of an invisible force — a force which is dual in its action, and its dual action being balanced at a central point which is neither centrifugal nor centripetal, but where the two are one. And if this balance were overcome by either form of force, the visible universe would vanish like a shadow.

Just as the art of *measuring* deals with the visible numerals, so the art of *counting* or numbering treats of the invisible numerals. All counting is based on the Quarterni, 1, 2, 3, 4. Their sum is 10, ten tens are 100, and so on to infinity. All the operations of arithmetic are also based on the first four, viz., addition, subtraction, multiplication, division. But counting cannot be separated from something to count. The elements which comprise the earth's surface and atmosphere combine only according to count.[112] Take e. g. the two invisible gases, oxygen and hydrogen. They combine and form water only according to the number *two*. And, moreover, this combination is *audible* at the instant at which it becomes visible.

This number *two* holds the balance of power. It represents the point which is neither oxygen nor hydrogen, but where the two are *one*, and I have only to overcome this polarity to cause the visible water to vanish into two invisible gases. But what is true of water is true of all compounds comprising the earth's surface. Destroy the numeral condition and the visible vanishes. Even the *diamond*, the hardest known substance, heated in oxygen gas, burns to carbonic acid, and carbonic acid at the ordinary atmospheric temperature is a transparent, colorless gas.

In order to determine the relation of measuring to counting, I turn to my imprisoned ray of sunlight, pictured on the wall in seven different colors, viz.:

Red, Orange, Yellow, Green, Blue, Indigo, Violet.
1   2   3   4   5   6   7

Now the odd numbers, 1, 3, 5, 7, are certainly different gradations of *refraction* from the white back to the white, completing the circle. But 2, or orange, which is between red and yellow, *reflects* both red and yellow, and is thus a mixture or compound of the two. Again, 4, or green, reflects both yellow and blue; 6, or indigo, reflects both blue and violet. Thus I see that the odd numbers 1, 3, 5, 7, signify different gradations of the centrifugal force or straight line, while the even numbers, 2, 4, 6, are gradations of the centripetal force, or crooked line. *Counting expresses gradations of measuring.*

But what is true of the seven colors is equally true of the seven notes :

1   2   3   4   5   6   7

Red, Orange, Yellow, Green, Blue, Indigo, Violet.

C   D   E   F   G   A   B

c, e, g, b, (superscript with 1,3,5,7) are different gradations of refraction from the octave to the octave, while d, f, a (superscript 2,4,6) are reflected tones, corresponding in quality to the colors they represent.

The exquisite primary cord 1, 3, 5, or C, E, G, is Red, Yellow and Blue manifested to my consciousness through my ear instead of my eye. So every conceivable cord and combination of tone and color can be written out in figures, until I am led to exclaim: Sound is color made audible; and color is sound made visible ! My eye and my ear are avenues to my consciousness of the two halves of a unity. In order to determine whether the sense of touch is the avenue to my consciousness of the unity of the two halves, I next give my attention to the *Tangible.*

LESSON IV.

RAY-MENT— TANGIBLE.

I might have been born blind, and yet been able to determine the meaning, the harmony, and to a certain degree, even the color of objects about me, by means of touch. I might have been born deaf, and yet been able to determine the meaning of words, and the harmonies of sound from touch and sight. I might have been born with only the sense of touch, yet have attained to a higher and truer knowledge of the world in which I live than many about me endowed with five senses.

But without the sense of touch I could not maintain my terrestrial existence. When feeling goes, life of the visible body goes too. Touch is, then, the vital sense of the terrestrial body.

When I push my hand against a stone, or thrust it into water, or pass it through the air, I am conscious of different degrees of *resistance*. And I classify objects about me according to the different degrees of resistance which they offer to my touch. The air, when it offers no resistance to my touch, is unperceived, so without resistance there is no *touch*.

But what is resistance? Resistance is simply force, an invisible action and reaction, which is expressed by, and can be determined from, numbers, *e. g.*, the resistance of water is expressed by the number 2. I have only to overcome the polarity or equilibrium expressed by this numeral to render the water, which was tangible, tangible no longer.

But what can be done in the case of water is also possible in the case of the most seemingly immovable solids of the earth. By means of burning glasses the sun's rays can be collected to a central point, or focus, and heat obtained sufficient to change solid rocks into liquid flames. And thus I come to realize that the tangible is tangible only according to certain definite conditions which correspond exactly with the conditions according to which the *Visible* is visible and the *Audible* is audible.

Upon comparing the three forms of rayment still further, I am convinced that the visible, and the audible, likewise, are perceivable by me, only by means of *Resistance*. The one is resistance of light vibrations, or radiations, and the other is resistance of breadth vibrations, or radiations. So that sight and sound can be said to be forms of *Touch*. Touch thus represents the point where sight and sound are one.

All sensation may then be called touch, or *Resistance* expressed in different degrees. The sense of touch (ordinarily so called) expresses the first degree, or most actual and living contact; sound, the second degree; vision, the third degree, or most remote and external contact.

Thus, to hear and see flames may affect me very agreeably, but the effect of touch would be quite the contrary. Yet the flames come in contact with my consciousness as truly in the one case as in the other.

The fact of the *unity* of sensation is well illustrated in the case of a child. It is never satisfied with simply looking at an object. It must *see* with its fingers as well as its eyes. And shakes or drops the object in order to *see* with its ears also.

Now since I have decided that this terrestrial ray-ment is only an inverted reflect of a celestial ray-ment, or thoughtment, I must strictly apply this fact in the case of sensation.

This *resistance*, comprised under the three forms of visible, audible and tangible sensation; this purely terrestrial touch : this my means of communication with the external world, or terrestrial minds about me, is simply an inverted reflect of a higher sense of *Touch*, of a *Resistance* to an interior or celestial world of Thoughts and *Minds* (since thoughts imply minds).

If I have hitherto been entirely unconscious of this interior three-fold sense, it is because my attention has been so taken up solely with external resistance that the interior resistance has been unobserved.

But when I do observe this interior resistance I find that, in its development, my experience corresponds to that of the child in the case of its exterior sensation. *I see first with my fingers.* This is the interpretation of bodily suffering. Body first responds to this thought resistance. But as I advance in knowledge and acquire this thought resistance through the other avenues of touch, thought vibrations, or radiations, which, like the flames, now cause me acute suffering, will become a source of most wonderful knowledge and understanding as soon as I can hear them and see them instead of simply feeling them. Then, what now prostrates me with physical suffering will become to me the greatest possible source of power and wisdom.

But before I can raise my interior and true sense of touch to the celestial plane, I must first pass through a terrestrial plane of thought. I am encompassed round about by a dense atmosphere of absorbing *cares*, in traffic, and in social and political life. I must *feel* my way through this earthly atmosphere before I can reach a higher realm of Thought. First, I feel my way with touch in the first degree, which means suffering; second, with touch in the second degree, by means of which I begin to observe a harmony and meaning in the confused din and squabble about me; and finally, with touch in the third degree, whence my eyes are gradually opened, and *seeing* for the first time in my life, I come to know how to see less with my fingers and more with my ears and my eyes.

Thus I come to discern the relation of terrestrial body and mind to celestial body and mind.

Reflected body and its three-fold sense is simply *raiment*, or *garment*, or *visible expression* for the celestial body, or *soul*.

Finite, or earthly, or reflected mind is the *food* or nourishment for the *soul*, by means of which the soul after *hungering*, *eating* and *assimilating* the husks of finite thought, returns to its Father's house, to be fed with the heavenly bread and *staff* of life, and to enter upon the celestial heritage.

This great truth of my celestial heritage is first *refracted* to my consciousness through the tear-drops of suffering, then afterwards *reflected,* by means of numbers and harmony, to my vision.

Touch is the refractory medium through which the *Divine Ray* is transmitted to my consciousness, while the medium refracts outwardly, the *Ray* is a *rod* of correction, but when it refracts back toward its celestial source, it is the *staff* which comforts.

The Tangible is thus the point of equilibrium between the Visible and the Audible, the vital point of radiation, while radiation itself, or motion, changes sensation from the plane of reflected body to the plane of reflected Intellect, for to the second *spire* or coil of the *Serpent.*

LESSON V.

FOOD— HUNGER.

The polar opposite of touch is desire; and, although touch and desire cannot be separated the one from the other, yet I at once observe a very important and significant distinction. Touch, I cannot disconnect from bodily sensation; Desire, I cannot disconnect from mind — the purely finite or reflected mind.

Bodily sensation brings me in contact with the infinite wonders of the phenomenal universe, and spontaneous with this contact occurs the desire to experience and to know the reality back of this phenomenal — its meaning, and its purpose.

The way by which I am to reach this experience and knowledge is, obviously, very direct, if I but follow the straight and narrow path already marked out viz., as the phenomenal is an inverted and left-sided copy of the real; as external sensation also bears this relation to interior sensation, then must the desire connected with external sensation be also only an inverted and left-sided copy of a *Desire* which is interior, or esoteric. In other words, the interior sense of touch implies the esoteric desire, just as external touch implies external desire.

In order to reach this *esoteric* desire, I must, indeed, start from the *exoteric* desire — the outward doth from the inward roll — and the inward dwells in the inmost soul. I must possess myself of the knowledge which only can be bought by experience, and which comes from direct contact with the phenomenal. *But* I must accept the experience of sensation and desire only as a means of knowing reality — the *exoteric* must always be my ladder to the *esoteric*. The *Visible* must simply reflect to me images of objects which in themselves are entirely beyond my range of sight; from the *Audible* I must learn to detect the counts of the *Still Voice*; while the rod of the *Tangible*, with its two ends of pleasure and pain, must truly "Feed full my sense for a while;" until balancing the rod and finding the point of equilibrium between pleasure and pain, I attain to the *interior vision*, "The sight that my soul yearns after."

To refuse the experiences of bodily sensation and desire is to refuse ray-ment and food to the soul; and thus to deprive the soul of its only means of development toward final perfection.

But, to be deceived by these images — to accept the mere reflections for the realities themselves — is the *fundamental error*, or, in other words, the *fatal sin of Idolatry*. No matter whether I call it *error*, or whether I call it *sin*, the thing in itself, independent of what I may call it, is *Idolatry*.

Therefore, although I must diligently till the soil of this terrestrial ray-ment and its sensations, the fruit must not be consecrated to the idols themselves, but must be brought as an offering and sacrificed to the *true desire* of soul.

Now, if I say the irrevocable penalty of Idolatry is *Disease* and *Death*, I but state in other words the fact that *Disease* and *Death* are logical results of calling inverted shadows the entities they *are* not and *cannot* be.

The fact in itself acts quite independent of whatever I may choose to call it. Idolatry is not pacified with the term *sin* any more than by the word *error*.

As long as I am an *Idolator*, I am subject to disease and death in spite of the creed to which I may subscribe, in spite of the benevolence and morality I may practice, or even in spite of the drugs I may swallow and the laws of hygiene I may observe.

Nor is this death penalty of Idolatry canceled with once meeting its decrees; on the contrary, it means innumerable deaths for me, until, by my own insight, I renounce the Idolatry of shadow worship, and turn to the *Living Ray-ality*.

Yet the requisite *insight*, together with the necessary power of choice, do not reside in the finite mind itself. They cannot be separated from it, but their true seat is in the *soul*.

That consciousness possessed by the finite mind and its desires (hungers), together with its seeming power of choice, are but illusory reflects of *Soul* (true consciousness), and true *Freedom*. Soul is the *true Ego*, while the consciousness possessed by finite mind and its desires is *reflected* ego. So also in this power of choice which I possess, I must distinguish between a *true* and a *reflected* Freedom.

Now, this true ego is the central point of my four-fold system as a whole; body is raiment to this ego, and, just as I must needs have many garments in the course of my earth life, so must the true ego require innumerable robes in its long course of development toward perfection. Finite mind is food to the true ego, and also, just as my finite mind and its hungers is not in itself developed by one meal of victuals, so the true ego requires for its nourishment during its long process of growth the food supplied by innumerable finite existences. (In mineral, vegetable, animal and lastly man.) In other words, *the true ego is only developed by means of innumerable incarnations.* Herein is the mystery of birth and death.[113]

Of my staff of finite mind, desire is the head; and just as the staff must follow the course of the head in its revolutions, so the *exoteric* desire leads the whole staff in downward spirals to the very depths of the shadows; but the *esoteric* desire leads in upward spirals toward the celestial light.

As the polar opposite of desire is action, action must then be the foot of my staff of finite mind.

But esoteric desire of the finite mind is only another term for hunger of soul, and just as desire implies action, so hunger implies eating.

Esoteric desire and action of the finite mind are *hunger* and *eating* of the *true Ego.*

LESSON VI.

FOOD— EATING.

Since desire is either true desire or reflected desire, exoteric or esoteric, then must the action implied by desire be either exoteric action or esoteric action.

Accordingly, studying action as dual, as true action and reflected action, I first observe that the two forms must, of necessity, be exactly contradictory. This is implied in the relation itself of a reflect to the object it reflects. Action on the plane of finite thought moves in a diametrically opposite direction from action on the plane of the celestial. And as long as the finite acts unconscious of the higher plane, which it simply contradicts (reflects), that power of choice which I seem to possess is, in truth, the exact contradictory of choice. It is only the choice of the winds and the tides, the times and the seasons, which obey the hidden law instead of coming and going as they themselves may choose.

As my eyes become opened to the relation of exoteric action to esoteric action, as expressed in the law of contradictories, the more evident it becomes to me, that the very actions, in the performance of which I was most certain of perfect power of choice, were the very ones in which I had absolutely no choice.

On this plane of the shadows I find that although I have eyes I see not, although I have ears yet I hear not, and although I *act* with seeming freedom, yet all my acts are contradictory; what I do with my right hand, that my left undoes, and what I affirm with my lips, that my heart denies; when I would walk in one direction my feet follow the opposite.

Thus I come to realize that the quality of all my action on the finite plane, though seemingly active, is in truth, passive. Accordingly I regard all finite action (exoteric action) as in its essence, *Passion*.

Again, action is always put forth as a means to obtain a given end. It is a reaching out toward, accordingly I must regard action as Offering, or *Oblation*, as well as *Passion*.

From this it directly follows that all my actions which have in view terrestrial aims, pleasures and possessions are offerings, or sacrifices made to idols (shadows). As long as in my desires I worship idols, all my acts must, of necessity, be oblations to my idols, for the desire and the act mutually imply each other. But, on the other hand, it also directly follows that as soon as my desires becomes esoteric all my actions will be offerings to the *living Ray-ality* instead of to shadow idols.

The ancient myth of Saturn feeding upon his own helpless offspring, is, I find, an exact type of my true ego, which is sustained and developed to maturity (im-mortality) by devouring its own reflected (mortal) images.

However, as long as I am an idolater, and my desires purely exoteric, I find that I, in my turn, act the part of Saturn to all beneath me in the plane of shadow. I desire, and seek my own comfort and welfare as paramount. If I am humane it is because I am enlightened enough to discern that thus I best secure my own ends. And even on the plane of body, while I continue to maintain my animal life at the expense of my animal kindred, I do so without perceiving that I thus have the distinctive mark which classifies me with the beast of prey tribe.

I deprive a helpless victim of the birthright to life for the sake of a mess of savory pottage, thus securing for myself both the birthright and pottage. And as I analyze my line of conduct still further, I find that this one act is a perfect type of every act of worldly wisdom and prudence.[114]

But the instant my desire becomes esoteric, the whole line of conduct is reversed and begins to move in the opposite direction. Action is no longer sacrifice of the higher to the lower, but becomes a series of oblation after oblation of the lower to the higher. Each act is the renunciation of a shadow for a true ray. Each step upon the ladder by which I mount from the exoteric to the esoteric is the crucifixion of a contradictory of truth.

Yet any ascetic practice I may adopt which merely aims to *restrain the external act*, while the desire still exists in full force, is as futile a performance as it would be for me to set myself to work to cut off one end of my staff and expect to have only one end left. I must not attempt the impossible, but must patiently set myself to work to balance my staff of desire and action, and not being discouraged with repeated failures, *persist*, sustained by the knowledge that the staff *can* be balanced, *that* there *is* a point of equilibrium between desire and act, and that upon this point I can step, in perfect security, to the higher plane. But if I try to step upon either end the staff will surely tip. It is only the point of equilibrium which will sustain my weight.

These *steps* are the true sacrifices by means of which I attain to my maturity. They are the *burnt* offerings of consumed shadows upon which the true ego feeds, until, accumulating the necessary strength, it will finally free itself wholly from the shadows and enter upon its celestial heritage. They are the offspring of Saturn, which will eventually possess themselves of their father's throne and power.

But *how* will they possess themselves of this power? Hunger and eating are polar opposites; now the equilibrium between hunger and eating, or the point where the two are *one*, is assimilation. The strength of my phenomenal body seemingly comes from the assimilation which follows eating. But this seeming fact is only a reflection of the seeming fact that the finite mind obtains its finite wisdom from its power of assimilating thought. While this seeming fact, in its turn, is but *reflection* of the *Truth* that the celestial *Power* of the true ego is attained through its assimilation of its own esoteric offspring, or its true *Sacrifices*.

LESSON VII.

FOOD— ASSIMILATING.

On the plane of body, assimilation occurs through the secretions, or fluids. On the plane of finite mind, the *mental picture* expresses the point of assimilation between mind and thought.

Now, the relation of finite mind to body is that of cause to effect. Finite mind symbolizes action; body, re-action; and since action and reaction are only different terms for refraction and reflection, it follows that all operations of body are reflected mental operations ; therefore, it also follows that all forms and conditions of secretions are reflected mental pictures.

In the case of finite mind, the mental picture is expressed outwardly by means of words, spoken or written, or through some of the arts.

In the case of body, the secretions (reflected mental pictures) expressed outwardly are bones, muscles, skin, etc.

Just so in the case of the globe I inhabit — its liquids (reflected mental pictures) expressed outwardly are its geological formation, its rocks, minerals, etc.

In order to clearly and fully grasp this relation, I will first analyze it by means of my staff, and then follow out its application in the case of a word.

(1.) The word in itself as external (visible or audible) is the *head* of my staff.

(2.) Its finite or reflected significance and force, is the *foot* of my staff.

(3.) My *experience* of the significance and force of the word is the point of balance between the external word and its internal force; and this experience is of different degrees, from a merely blind physical re-action up to the highest form *of consciousness*.

(4.) The true, celestial force and meaning of a word is *motion*, which completes the *Quarterni*.

Now I will apply this analysis in the case of the word which is expressed outwardly, or phenomenally, as *arsenic*.

(1.) Arsenic is a weapon of a cold, steel grey color, and of a glittering lustre. This metal is the visible expression of a *reality* which on the plane of finite mind I term *Calumny*. *Arsenic* is the steel grey, glittering weapon of the assassin *Calumny*, and the metal in itself no more destroys than the weapon can slay apart from the hand of the assassin.[115]

Arsenic destroys bodily tissues and functions for the very simple reason that it cannot be separated from the thought which it represents. It cannot come in contact with my sense of touch without suggesting to my mind, and then to my body, the thought of which it is an inverted reflect. It makes no difference whether my sense of touch comes in contact with the symbol through my stomach or through my eyes, it is the *thought* which slays, and not its reflected image.

Neither does it make the slightest difference in the result that I did not *know* my mind was acting, and my body re-acting, to the thought Calumny; for I *know* next to nothing of the majority of the thoughts which pass and repass through my mind, either of their true meaning, or of their connection, or how they come and where they go.

(2.) But the visible effect of swallowing arsenic upon my body only expresses a more real effect, on the plane of finite mind, of the assassin Calumny upon my whole terrestrial usefulness and existence.

(3.) However, when I grasp the meaning of the law of contradictories, and begin to know the esoteric life, I gradually come to know that the more powerless I am rendered on the lower plane, the more do I gain power on the true plane, if I but know how to use it.

(4.) As my *experience* of the true force and significance of the word is raised toward true *consciousness*, I also begin to discern the celestial force of the word Calumny, and finally behold, in the assassin, only a left-handed and inverted redeemer.

But what is true of this one word is true of all words. The whole universe can be regarded as words in different degrees of evolution, just as it can be considered thought-rays in different degrees of manifestation. I must first learn the names of these words, then I must combine words into phrases, then into sentences. But, after I become a proficient in reading, it is a long time before I can grasp even the external (reflected) significance of what I read. And only after most profound study and experience of the external do I come, finally, to grasp the law of contradictories, through which I gain the esoteric vision that enables me to discern the true and right-sided reality even while my exoteric eye sees only its inverted reflection. This whole process expresses the various degrees of *reading*, and esoteric reading is the *assimilation* of the true ego.

From this analysis I observe a solemn import in the use of words. No matter how ignorantly I may use them, I must render an account of my use ; for the word cannot be disconnected from its significance any more than the reflect can be separated from the object it mirrors, or *re*action can exist apart from action.

No matter how I may regard words, just as surely as I call upon them with my lips, just so surely do I evoke their true significance and force, which will act in sublime indifference to any conventional opinion I may chance to hold of their meaning. Words will follow the force which impels them, and will rebound according to count. But when I become an esoteric reader and know the law of the action and the count of the rebound, these words no longer rule me, but I rule words, until finally I *realize* the *power* which follows assimilation.

This power of assimilating contradictories which enables me to see in death only an inverted and left-sided reflect of Life; and also to see that birth and death are opposite ends of the same staff, is the light upon my path which leads to my celestial heritage. It is also the *illumination* by means of which this heritage is made visible to my esoteric sense.

But assimilation, in its highest degree, is the gestation and travail of that *new birth* which is neither birth nor death, but the *life eternal.*

LESSON VIII.

HOUSE— PROPORTION.

My staff of Consciousness has two ends and a point of equilibrium, i. c, exoteric consciousness, esoteric consciousness and soul (true ego), the invisible centre where the two ends are one. Consciousness, as a whole, is the tent, the covering, or *House* of the true ego; exoteric consciousness is the outer room; esoteric consciousness the inner room, while the soul itself is symbolized by the Hearth situated in the centre of the house between the two rooms.

Before proceeding upon this study of Consciousness, I must bear in mind the fact that I am now dealing with entities which are not palpable to the senses — Consciousness I cannot see, hear nor touch: it is a *House not made by hands*,[116] and to accept literally any of the terms employed in designating degrees and relations of consciousness will be to fall into the grossest error. And yet, since this present study is devoted to the exposition of the psychical basis of physical health, my study cannot go beyond the ground plan of this house; its elevation plan must be reserved for future study in Reality.

In my present study I can only consider my cloud celestial with reference to my cloud terrestrial, and not with reference to its relation with its celestial Sun and Source.

In the study of my cloud terrestrial, I have been dealing with Reflection and inverted Reflects; now, however, I must study my celestial heritage as Refraction, and true Refracts. And I must constantly bear in mind that, owing to the blindness of my esoteric vision, these true Refracts will at first seem to me upside down: but as my eyes are opened, *Refracts* will seem right side up, but *Reflects* will then, for the first time, seem in their true light as inverted.

The House of Consciousness, as a whole, must, therefore, be a true refraction of which my Ray-ment of Body was the inverted reflection.

Of my staff of Ray-ment, the *Visible* was the head; therefore, that which appeals to the eye in the case of House, or *Proportion*, must be the true refract, of which the Visible is the inverted reflect. The Proportion which appeals, through my exoteric vision, to my sense of harmony, is the external symbol of that *true Proportion* discernible only through my esoteric vision.

Proportion is commonly defined as an equality or equilibrium of ratios. And since it must consist of four terms, Proportion is the scales, or balance, of the Quarterni.

In the case of *body*, this balance is the equilibrium of the four elements, which results in the consciousness of physical proportion termed *Health*.

In the case of *finite mind*, this balance is the equilibrium of mind, thoughts, mental pictures and outward expression (in speech, in art, etc.), which results in the consciousness of mental proportion termed knowledge and power.

But on the true and larger plane it is the equilibrium of my celestial and terrestrial refraction and reflection, which results in the conscious possession and realization, on the part of the true ego, of its celestial heritage.

Now, the terrestrial reflection was dual; i. e., it consisted of action (finite mind) and a reaction (body). So the celestial refraction also consists of an action (a Ray, one with and inseparable from its Sun and Source), and a reaction (true ego). Accordingly, in order to clearly see and firmly grasp the relation of the dual reflection to its dual refraction, I state them thus: starting with the reflection, I represent body by a; finite mind by b; true ego by x; celestial Ray by y.

Now, since Proportion is an equilibrium of ratios, it directly follows from the nature itself of reflection and refraction that $a : b : : x : y$, or, body is to finite mind as the true eeo is to its celestial Ray.

Body (is to) finite mind (as) true ego (is to) Ray.

a   :   b   ::   x   :   y

Reflected Reflected   Refracted Refracted
re-action: action   :: re-action : action

a and *b* (body and finite mind) are the known terms of this proportion, x and y the unknown terms; and the problem stated thus, $a : b : : x : y$, represents the true equilibrium between reflection and refraction, and at the same time states the reason that $a : b$, as it is, be*cause x :y*, as it is. But when I wish to solve the problem I transpose the unknown terms to the first member of the equation, and the known to the second member of the equation, or, turn the left hand to the right, thus, $x : y : : a : b$, *an instinctive acknowledgement of the fact that the known is the inverted and left-sided copy of the unknown.*

The word ratio is from the Latin *radius* (ray or rod), therefore in its derived significance a ratio is a rod, and proportion is accordingly an equilibrium of rods, and thus is the true meaning expressed in the derivation, since proportion is equilibrium between reflected rods (rays) and refracted rods.

This equilibrium of rods is always a problem capable of solution, although one requiring skill and patience. The value, meaning, and force of *x*, or *true ego*, is always the point to be ascertained.

Here, again, I notice that the very symbol itself (the *x*) which I have instinctively employed to designate the true ego expresses, by its form of cross, the equilibrium of two rods. Thus, not only is proportion itself a statement of the problem of the soul, but also the term itself, which stands for soul, states this momentous problem.

Reflecting still further, I find that proportion, as the equilibrium of reflected rods and refracted rods, states and solves all the problems of light, heat, sound and motion, and thus I come to regard the whole phenomenal universe as but a continuous statement and re-statement of this problem of the soul.

But I have just found that each statement, in itself, is dual ; that at the same time, or together with the statement, there is also a re-statement, or *reason why*, implied in the statement itself, I.e. the statement also implies the solution ; or, *to state is to solve*, thus,

(as) (because)

a : b :: x : y   a : b :: x : y

Statement.   *Solution.*

The statement implies knowledge, while the solution (re-statement) expresses faith. But the equilibrium between this statement and its re-statement is the anchor by means of which the true ego realizes its Ray-ment, or *House* of consciousness as the refracted reality, of which its Ray-ment of *bodily sensation* was the inverted reflection.

LESSON IX.

HOUSE— DOOR.

Between the outer and inner rooms of my House of Consciousness there is a door, which swings out or in. The name of this door is Doubt. When it swings out, the counts of its vibrations are audible to my external ear; but when it swings in, the counts are audible only to my esoteric ear.

This double nature of my door is expressed in its very name; for doubt is derived from two Greek words which signify to *go two ways*, and to doubt is, very literally, to be in the mental and physical condition of trying to walk in two opposite directions at the same time.

However, from *doubt* — from this attempt to walk in two opposite directions at the same time — is produced all mental *action*, which ultimately results in knowledge. Doubt is the only door through which I can ever reach absolute *certitude*.

As long as I do not doubt, but accept everything as it appears on the outside, taking for granted the seeming for the real, the door between me and knowledge is closed and locked. But the moment I begin to doubt the door begins to swing, and it swings out, creaking and grating, and forces me away from the very knowledge I would seek; while I, deceived by the sound, think, because the door is opening, and because I am listening to the counts, that I am thus acquiring truth, while I am, really, only acquiring the contradictory of truth Thus I who sincerely seek truth, partake only of its inverted reflect, and, thereby, deceived and bewildered, I become a victim of all manner of delusions, and *fearful* of shadows, until finally the door swings clear back against the wall, and can go no further. The door has swung wide open, and to doubting was due the whole mental activity by which this result was accomplished.

In its course of outward movement the door has described a semicircle. There is but one way to complete the circle, viz., the door must swing back again, and then swing over the threshold into the inner, and hitherto unknown room of my house, until it reaches the wall again on the inner side; then the circle will be complete.

Doubt has opened wide the door, and manifested the whole process of the movement which described the outer semicircle. Now, the *determination to complete* and to *know* the other half of the circle is the exact contradictory of doubt. Determination *reverses* the movement of the door. It begins to swing in.

To determine is, therefore, to reverse doubt, not to abandon it; for, manifestly, determination without previous line of doubt to follow back upon must surely end in my finding myself just where I started, i. e. y before a closed and locked door.

The way to reverse doubt is to, at once and unreservedly, doubt all that doubt has previously accepted as real, what doubt has hitherto decided to be unreal. Thus will I possess myself of the key which will force the door to swing over its latch without locking. But I must swing the door clear open, and describe the inner semicircle, before I can myself pass in and consciously possess myself of the treasures of this esoteric consciousness.

In geometry, the word *term* signifies the *point* and the *line*, and to *de-term-ine* is to limit by means of the point and the line. Accordingly, to doubt and to determine is the process b means of which I arrive at the true meaning of the point and the line. *Doubt* is the form of force which causes the door to swing, or strike out from the centre of equilibrium, or, the centrifugal force; while *Determination* is the form of force which draws back to the centre, or, centripetal force. Now, when these two forms of force are in perfect equilibrium, my door will describe the perfect circle. But before that, in my actual experience while developing this circle, this larger line is in itself marked out by an incessant pendulum-like swing, first back, then forth, of the door, and so on — an infinitely zigzag line, and a continuous tick-tack of count, the counts varying according to the longer or shorter swing of the door. And these counts express gradations of *doubt* and *determination*. This I also found to be the relation between the two forms of numerals, or, counting and measuring.

Doubt has led to a mental activity which has resulted in the accumulation of facts, or knowledge of the external construction of my circle. Determination is the re-action against doubt,which will ultimately force the door back and within.

The relations of doubts and determinations is that of cogs and grooves, and without the two the wheel could not revolve; *i. e.*, doubts and determinations are polar opposites which mutually imply each other. Just so my outer semicircle, when completed, must be the polar opposite of the inner semicircle, and since the two mutually imply each other, when I know the external I also know what the inner must be.

The name, Doubt, which I have given my door, since it signifies to go two ways, implies both doubt and determination in itself. However, as doubt is the first act which drives the door away from the inner room, and determination impels it back into my esoteric consciousness, I now give my door two names to designate the direction in which it swings. Thus, when swinging out I call it Doubt, when swinging in I call it Determination, for it is determination which forces the door in — tears it open.

Now the first meaning of the word *door*, is to tear or break open, the same word also meaning to *pray* or to supplicate. Doubt is action, determination, re-action. Door, or true *prayer* is the point of equilibrium between the two.

As I carefully regard the nature of my consciousness, I find that in the day time I am actively absorbed with the external and phenomenal. But that at night, in sleep I pass to the re-active, or apparently unconscious state. Yet, if I awaken suddenly I am often conscious of having been interrupted in a train of thought; or of being recalled from distant lands and scenes which I was visiting in dreams.

By addition of motion to proportion (balanced rods), the form thus described builds me a spiral house. Also the two rooms described by the swinging of my door, marks out to my ear a circular house.

Proportion and *Door* express the same house of two rooms, the one to my esoteric *eye*, the other to my esoteric *ear*. Proportion and door symbolize the true refracts of which the visible and audible are the inverted reflects. Furthermore, Day and Night consciousness express the true refracts of color and sound sensation. *Day is night made visible. Night is day made audible.*

LESSON X.

HOUSE— HEARTH.

Since my house is spiral, the line between its two rooms is a diameter, or two radii (rods, rays). The door is one radius, the hearth is the other.

My hearth is the warmth giving vital centre. It is the point from whence the *Hearth-fire* radiates and permeates my whole house.

In my physical system, this vital centre is the heart, situated on the left side, while the lungs on the right, are the door which swinging incessantly back and forth, fans the life flame glowing on my hearth, or in my heart. Thus I see that on the *reflected* plane, my hearth is my heart, and examining the two words I see the heart (h) is heart with an aspirate (a spira) added. And this addition of the breathing which changes heart to hearth signifies the inseparable unity of *Hearth and Door* as well as the inseparable unity of *heart and breathing.*

Hearth and door as a unity are a diameter, as polar opposites, they are two radii. Now the point of equilibrium between the two radii is the point of radiation, the centre of reflected (physical) life, the centre of refracted life which is consciousness. And strangely enough the word *H-ear-th* expresses all this in its formation. The two breathings are the polar opposites, the radii; while the word ear means to shoot, to dart, to ray.

And this point of radiation, is also the centre of my whole house; for, the revolution of these radii about the centre describe the circle which bounds my whole house. And since my door and my hearth extend from the floor to the ceiling, they must in their revolution, describe a spiral or cylindrical form of house. My house is thus my tower. And since to shoot, to ear is the centre, the ear of corn is, very truly, the symbol of my house, as my tower. But my house is consciousness, therefore *consciousness* is my tower, my strength and my defense.

Just as the ear of corn symbolizes the external form of my house, so the *listening ear* expresses the esoteric reality of consciousness. Now ear implies voice, just as heart implies breathing, just as hearth implies door. *Voice* is sound thrown out by *breath*, therefore *ear*: voice: : hearth : door. And this proportion must both state, and solve all problems of consciousness involving the relation of hearth to door.

The *listening ear* is the ear leaning, inclining, stretching out toward, or, in other words, it is the *resisting ear*. It is the ear *resisting*, or re acting against the vibrations thrown out by the voice of my door. List and lust are the same in derivation, — list is the resistance to the true vibrations, lust is the resistance to the reflected vibrations.

Resistance, in itself, is dual, *e. g.* in the case of external sensation; unless my consciousness re-acts against the action offered by the polarity of external objects, I experience no sense of touch.

Now as long as my consciousness is wholly occupied in external and phenomenal resistance, it knows only the voice and language of exoteric consciousness. But after I learn from experience of the visible, audible and tangible, to comprehend the relation of reflection to refraction, I come to see, from proportion what must be the relation of the hearth to the door of my house of consciousness, *i. e., since*, on the physical (reflected) plane, the relation of eye to light vibrations, of ear to voice, of heart to breathing, but express different degrees of resistance, or forms of the sense of touch, therefore, on the refracted plane, the relation of esoteric hearth to esoteric door expresses the true refract, of which the three- fold sense of resistance is the inverted reflect.

And, accordingly, if I would know the eso-teric voice of my door, and acquire the language of its esoteric breathing, so as to discern its relation to the esoteric raying (earing) of my hearth, then I must combine Knowledge and Faith as shown in Proportion.

Knowledge is the insight into the equilibrium of ratios; Faith is the trust that the *refraction* which I cannot see, is the cause of the reflection which I do see; thus Faith is the *discerning eye*.

Prayer is the trust that the inaudible vibration is the *cause* of the audible vibration. And this inaudible vibration is the *still voice* which the *listening ear doors* (prays) *open, — hears.*

Realizing (ray-izing) is the trust that this vital spark of consciousness, impalpable to my exoteric resistance, is the *cause* of the flame smouldering on my hearth of heart. And this vital spark is tangible to the resisting hearth, — the pure heart.

The discerning eye sees the celestial Ray, the listening ear *communes* with It, — the resisting heart consciously and vitally *realizes* It.

This Ray is one with and inseparable from its celestial Sun and Source; — this Ray is a Thought of the Infinite Mind, and one with Infinite Mind. So that when I see the Ray, I also see the Sun, for the sun and its rays are one; when I know the Thought I also know the *Mind*, for mind and thoughts cannot be separated.

Mind and Thought-rays become one, or, are assimilated, through mental pictures. Therefore, this pure hearth of heart, this vital centre of consciousness, when it resists, or reacts against the celestial Thought-ray, not only becomes assimilated with the Thought-ray itself, but also brings to a *vital focus*, a mental picture of Infinite Mind.

My true ego, my soul is, therefore, a mental picture of the Infinite Mind in process of expression. And it takes many and hard lines to bring this mental picture to a focus, and to emancipate it from its own inverted reflections.

The Divine Artist acts through the Thought- ray. And when my soul consciously *re-acts*, or responds, the work goes on swiftly. Moreover, since thought and mental picture mutually imply each other, just as mind implies thought, therefore, I am one with Infinite Mind as soon as I *consciously accept* and *realize* the *fact* of *Inseparableness.*[117]

An appeal to consciousness is always ultimate. The sensations of my body, and the desires of my terrestrial mind, are the undeniable facts of my consciousness, therefore to solve any problem of soul implied in the statement a : b : : x : y is a very simple process of *elimination;* for I always have the two following- equations from which to compare and substitute the value of *x*: Body [a : b : : sensation : y] finite mind [a : b : : desire : y But I know that to realize this inestimable value of x will be to cast out the errors of my desires, and to heal the diseases of my sensations; for the reflection must correspond to the refraction. And not only my own errors and diseases, but also those of other souls slumbering in their inner rooms of consciousness. For within every inner room there glimmers a celestial Thought-ray of Infinite Mind. And within the unity of this Infinite Mind our true consciousnesses all move and have their being.

To enter within this inner room and to realize its inseparable unity with the celestial Mansions of all consciousness, is to reverse Night and Day, and to awaken and find how soundly I have been asleep amid the inverted shadows of the true Aurora.

LESSON XI.

HEARTH-FIRE— RAY.

Drawing near my Hearth I now regard the fire growing upon its shrine, in order to learn from thence, of the celestial ray which transmutes the flame offered at the Altar of the heart into Soul.

These dancing and gleaming flames upon my Hearth are, indeed, very literally transformed sunlight, and it was as a perpetual reminder of this fact, that, in olden times, in case the hearth- fire should, by mischance, go out it would be relighted from sunlight by collecting rays to a focus. So in studying these glowing embers, I am but studying inverted sunlight, while sunlight in its turn is but reflected Thought-light. What first attracts my attention is the fact of *motion* — without this motion, or radiation, the entire manifestation of light and heat disappears.

Motion is an inseparable factor of this fire which consists of polar opposites of fire and rays, and a point which is neither fire nor rays, but where the two are one, — the point where they constantly balance from one to the other in an endless circle.

Just so motion cannot be separated from mind and thoughts, any more than thoughts can exist apart from mind. In the case of mind I term this motion *reasoning* (derived from radius, rod), and thus reasoning is radiation both in meaning and derivation.

Even in the case of my staff which I designate as inanimate, were it not for a certain degree of motion it would not exist at all, it would vanish entirely from my sight. Thus, it is visible because it re-acts against light-vibrations. It is tangible because of certain equilibriums of action and re-action commonly termed attraction and repulsion.

Thus I see that *motion, radiation, reasoning* and *existence*, are all forms of *Ray-ing*, and ray-ing is the inseparable fourth element, or *Quarterni* in every *Unity*. Every Unity is an inseparable Duality, Trinity and Quarterni.

Although motion *cannot* be separated from unity, duality and trinity, yet I must distinguish between it and the other elements in order to comprehend the nature of *Force*, or Ray-ing, before I can divine its meaning, and realize its presence upon the altar of my *Hearth*.

The ray-ing of these flames before which I hold my hands, is of two kinds, viz.: For every ray-ing out, there is a ray-ing back. Different gradations of the ray-ing back but correspond to gradations of the ray-ing forth. Action and re-action are equal, or, in other words, there is an equilibrium between the forms of ray-ing.

At this point of equilibrium between the two, i. e., by the union of the two, are formed all manner of figures, mathematical, fantastic and beautiful. And as I closely watch them, I even discern the colors; now a dart of red, now a dart of blue, flashes of purple, and of gold.

But since flames are only inverted sunlight, every ray of light, therefore, also carries its prism with it, *i. e.*, its re-active form of force is its prism by means of which, through infinite equilibriums of its infinite gradations, it images forth infinite colors and forms.

Now I have already seen that every equilibrium, from the lowest gradation to the highest is a statement and re-statement of the problem of the Soul. Therefore each and every gradation, must, in itself, be a statement and re-statement of some different degree and phase of the general statement. And at once the whole visible universe looms up before me, no longer vague, chaotic and meaningless, but as a sublime universal language, which appeals, through sensation, to my whole nature.

(1.) Each vibration, and shade of *color*, is a reflected vibration and shade of Thought, of which it is a polar opposite, and from which it cannot be separated. So that when I once possess the key which translates the symbol to its thought, I am never at the mercy of a blind chance, but read according to an unalterable law. And each prismatic color, not only reflects a thought, but the seven together are spokes of a wheel, which by their *relation* to each other by their difficult gradations of refractions and reflections, reflect various thought relations. And moreover this wheel when re- volved at a certain velocity blends the seven colors into the pure white light, — and this also expresses a *thought*.

(2.) Each vibration of *sound*, but speaks to my listening ear in this same universal language. It *pronounces* the words spelt out to my eyes.

(3.) Through the resistance of *touch* this universal language becomes a vital, *living* reality to me. I not only see and hear, but I *feel* it throughout every nerve and fibre of my body. I *sensibly realize* myself as an inseparable member of the written word, perhaps only as a punctuation mark, yet in some way inseparably connected with the *sense* of the whole.

Touch implies desire, and passing from sensation to the second spire, or coil of my nature. I see at once, from the very necessities of finite desire, action and the assimilation of the two, that this universal language is a drama in which I am a blind puppet, obeying a hidden law of entrances and exits (births and deaths), and in which I but repeat a speech as pronounced to me, trippingly on the tongue, with no more conception of the plot of the play, and the real purpose for which it is enacted, than had Hamlet's players of the deep and hidden purpose for which he employed them.

But at length my consciousness passes the curve of the third coil of my spiral nature, and grasps the equilibrium of ratios, and combines the knowledge and faith which mutually imply each other, into a statement, — a statement which is also a solution of the esoteric sense of this great drama.

As I come to understand the external construction of this universal language, I see that our modern printing press is but an adaptation on the finite plane, of the principle according to which the Infinite Mind has published abroad throughout the universe, his divine thoughts and purposes. Therefore, to know my part, I must first learn the letters and words as they seem, then learn to read them upside down, and from right to left.

In the second place I must learn the exoteric *meaning* and *action* of my part in the drama. And here, as before, the *Ray of Light* is my clew of thread, which alone reveals the path through the labyrinth of bewildering shadows, to the abode of the *Minotaur* of finite desire and action. For the fabulous beast *Minotaur*, which was fed by the sacrifice of the choicest Athenian youths, but personifies the finite, or earthly mind, with its idol worship, — with its sacrifices and oblations of the higher nature to the lower. And this Minotaur must be slain by the *true Theseus*, before I can start out to *know* and *act* my part in the esoteric drama.[118]

The Ray is, therefore, first, in itself, the entire alphabet of the universal language. For, by its two forms of force, and point of equilibrium, it furnishes the point and lines according to which the whole visible universe is pictured out to my senses.

The Ray is, second, in itself, the fire (inverted sunlight), — the fuel, the father, the food of sensation, in its search after the Minotaur. Food and father are the same in derivation. And the finite mind is indeed the father of the body, in that it provides and cares for all its demands. But the finite mind is also the father or food of the Soul during the period of apprenticeship to the *Shadows*.

It is the reflected father of the Soul, and from it the Soul must learn of its celestial Father. Every time one finite mind goes out in the appearance called death, then the Soul re-kindles its finite food (fuel) from its celestial Father, or Thought-ray, and goes on anew, to learn its part in the drama, until I come to discern this celestial Ray in my heart, and realize this vital spark of consciousness as re-acting (responding) to it as its celestial Father. Then is the Ray the force by which I solve the meaning of the words about me; and divine their significance in the great drama. Then finally will *consciousness* be transmuted into *Soul*, qualified to enact its part in the larger drama, since having become one with its own celestial Father, it is also one with the *Father of All Lights*.

LESSON XII.

HEARTH-FIRE— IMAGES.

These mysterious forms which are constantly appearing and vanishing amid the flames glowing on my Hearth next claim my attention, — these faces, beautiful or weird, which suddenly gleam with an intelligence that I am rarely quick enough to interpret, ere the glance has melted into another expression, and assumed another face.

I have already seen that these images occur at the point of equilibrium between the two forms of force, or, the point where polar opposites are one.

Consciousness is, therefore, the *focus* where form, or images, is made clear, — made *manifest*. The word manifest at once interests me. The primary sense of the word man, manna, manes, is *image, form, shade*; festu was a small staff used to point out letters to children when learning to read, therefore the first meaning of man and festu joined together in the word *man-i-fest* evidently is to point out, or make clear the image, form, man, manna, manes. And this I take to be the object, or purpose of *all manifestation*, viz., to bring to a vital focus the divine image of Soul. Accordingly I regard images as of four degrees, or classes, the first two being reflected and terrestrial, the last two being refracted and celestial.

(1)   (2)   (3)   (4)

Man : Manes : : Soul : Manna.

(1.) Man, or body, is the external and visible expression of the image.

(2.) My present finite mind is a *manes* in process of expression.

(3.) Soul is a mental picture (image) of the Infinite Mind in process of development.

(4.) The celestial Thought-ray of Infinite Mind is the Manna, True Food, or Father of the Soul.

For every thought of my finite mind there is an accompanying mental picture, existing, so to speak, in my own mental light, and held at a focus by my consciousness. Now, obviously, if this mental picture is reflected to other minds within the range of my mental light, this mental picture will be mirrored on their screen, or tent of consciousness, and since mental picture can-not be separated from thought, their minds will also think my thought. This illustrates the way all thoughts come and go; for all minds are factors of an inseparable Unity, and are, therefore, in a constant state of action and reaction.

Now while my senses are wholly absorbed in the external, I never consciously *discern* mental pictures. They are an entirely unrecognized factor in my mental machinery. And, in the present age, all inner vision is sternly remanded to the realm of fantasy as the next door to insanity, and proof positive of morbid conditions of body and mind. Therefore, if I would ever know the truth of the inner vision, I must endure the infamy of being one who dreams dreams, and sees visions. (However, a very little experience and reflection soon convinces me that the mutual polarity of thought and mental picture explains all phenomena of dreams, clairvoyance, premonitions, apparitions, etc., etc.)

I have already found that all finite action is dual, i. e., it is passion, and it is *oblation*. Now oblation is of various degrees.

(1.) Part of my daily actions are the sacrifices of the lower forms of life to maintain my own bodily existence. But in return for these acts, certain sacrifices are required at my hands. The scales of *Proportion* measure out to me just as I measure out to others, for every scrap and muscle of animal flesh which I take into my system is a pictured scroll of suffering, fear of death, and sense of deprivation of an heritage to life. These words my sense of touch reports faithfully to my consciousness, and I myself, in my turn, am a constant slave to these same fears and sufferings. Yet, I must pass through a long period of apprenticeship in sacrificing to these images until I learn the esoteric meaning of the word sacrifice upon this plane of my nature. Then I will be enabled to sustain my physical life upon the vegetables, grains and fruits of the Earth, which are more directly transformed sunlight, and thus symbolic of the celestial manna.[119]

(2.) The social or moral acts of my daily life are sacrifices to the manes. The Manes are the *shades* of the departed. They are the cast off reflects of the soul, — photographs of soul, existing in the magnetic light. And since they are photographs of true consciousness, they must partake, in a degree, of the living Ray-ality they reflect. And must, therefore, possess a terrestrial and finite consciousness, capable of communicating (through mental pictures) with other intelligences. These finite consciousnesses with which I am surrounded constantly reflect to me my own past thoughts and deeds, and thus impel me to perform again the same acts and deeds. If I strongly set myself to do right, then my acts are sacrifices to the good manes, but if I am selfish and cruel, then I sacrifice to the evil manes. But, more than this, just as I am in a most complex social relation with other minds about me, so are my manes, also, involved in this same complex relation with the manes of other minds. Moreover, just as these photographs (manes) reflect good or evil thoughts to me, so they also reflect diseased, and otherwise marked physical, peculiarities to me. So that if I would maintain my physical health, I must be able to discern these shades which hang unseemly pictures in my *House* of consciousness. I must tear down the evil manes, and hang up the good manes.

(3.) These sacrifices to the good manes are absolutely essential to my progress toward my realization of soul; for the manes feed upon my finite mind and body, just as I feed upon the lower forms of life. These sacrifices are the *third* form of oblations, i. e., they are offerings to *Soul*; for, the soul, in its turn, also feeds upon the manes.

(4.) The *fourth* form of oblation is that of the soul to its celestial *Manna*. And, although, while *embodied* I must practice all four forms of sacrifices, yet I can never catch a gleam of soul and its implied eternity without hence-forward directing my entire course of action (oblation) so as to partake of the *food* which is *mercy* and not *sacrifice*, — which is love and not suffering, and finally to sustain myself wholly upon the celestial *Manna*.

Now, the soul as a mental picture of Infinite Mind, is of divine origin, poor, sinless, and *perfect*, in that it contains within itself, in the germ, all that is eventually evolved. And its evolution is the result of its own inner force, united to that of its own *Thought-ray*. Time is the period of its process of expression, but the soul has eternity back of it, and before it.

And at the end of its time, — its great day of *Memory*, when the soul, freed from birth and death, is ready to collect together different earth lives as so many events in one great whole,[120] — and is waiting to put on its beautiful garments, so as to go and dwell forever with its Father, and enact its parts of the larger Drama, within the celestial Mansions; then the stern Judge *Minos* draws or pours, these robes, or manes, from out his *Urn*, and only such as are worthy of eternity can be strung as beads on memory's silver cord.

The soul can assume only such characters as are fitted to be enacted in the presence of divinity. And the manes which have in no way reflected the true ego, but only its *contradictory*, will go out in the outer darkness of nothingness. For as they exist only as contradictories of the source light, among the inverted shadows, they have failed to lay hold of the true refraction, which alone is entity, which is eternal life, and when the soul's light is indrawn from the terrestrial, to its celestial *Source*, these inverted reflections will be utterly dispelled.

However, until the end of time, it is possible, for even the contradictory manes to be *quickened*. For, just as it is possible for me, when the visible life of my friend goes out, to hold his manes, spellbound, and in agony, by my grief, just so it is possible for me who have *House, Food* and *Ray-ment* to shelter the home-less, to feed the hungry, and to clothe the naked. Thus can I rescue this manes, and herein is the oblation which is *Love and not suffering*. But the grief of despair is, in truth, a refined form of vivisection.

LESSON XIII.

HEARTH-FIRE— LAW.

yea : nay : : Yea : Nay.
The Law of Man-i-fest-ation, or of *pointing* out Images, is the Law of Contradictories.

Contradictory Opposites are inverted and left-sided reflections of Real or Polar Opposites. Polar Opposites *mutually imply* and *include* each other, while Contradictory Opposites *mutually deny* and *exclude* each other.

And just as it is impossible for me to walk in two opposite directions at the same time; just as it is impossible for me to affirm both of two Contradictions to be true and avoid mental chaos and nothingness, just so it is impossible for me to affirm the identity of Real Opposites and Contradictory Opposites, and avoid spiritual chaos and nothingness.

To grasp this distinction is to make the choice between the Real and the un-real, between Light and darkness, between Life and death, between the Eternal and the temporal, between *Wholeness* and chaos. And it is the spiritual insight implied in this choice which is so beautifully expressed in the myth of Ariadna's Clew of Thread. Ariadna's mystical clew of thread symbolizes this intuitive discerning of the relation of True Opposites to contradictory opposites which will lead the true Theseus safely through the mazes of the Labyrinth of inverted reflections, and enable him to destroy the Minotaur of sense and seeming.

The fact that Ariadna's twist of thread symbolizes this inner, intuitive *Ray*, is evident from the derivation of the word twist, as well as from the formation itself of a twist. Thus the Greek word *skiza* is a twist, a torch, a flame. Our word *scissors* is also derived from this same word.

Again, in its formation, a twist expresses the mystery of this *Law*, thus the twist is composed of two strands (each strand double), which are first twisted in opposite directions, then by being doubled back upon each other, the two strands fly magically into one manifestation.[121]

In the thread of light the *Law* is expressed in the dual, and yet unitary manifestation of refracted ray and its inverted reflected ray.

The scissors also expressed the Law in their construction of two blades fastened at the centre, by a point, or pin. When opened they image a cross, while the movement itself, of cutting, expresses the contradictories; i. e. the two blades come together and cut only as a result of the movement which forced them apart. This movement of the scissors is also the movement of the hand bellows, which impart breath to the flame.

The *thread* is the path in the Labyrinth; the torch is the light on the path; the *scissors* cut along the narrow thread which twists in and out amid the mazy shadows; while the three are all *one*. They are the *Parcae*.

In order to still further study the Law of Contradictories, I take the word *Health*, and its contradictory *Disease*. Following the Quarterni of word as already given in the lesson or assimilating, thus:

(1.) The outer expression of disease upon the body in various forms, is the external symbol of the word.

(2.) On the plane of finite mind, dis-ease is lack of ease resulting from the erroneous judgment of a finite Health apart from Infinite Wholeness.

(3.) My conscious experience of the word is the point of equilibrium between the finite and Infinite meaning of the word.

(4.) The true and celestial force and significance of the word completes the Quarterni, and Health would therefore be wholeness, completeness and perfection.

On the reflected, or finite plane, Health as ordinarily understood is, in truth, lack of wholeness, inasmuch as it is taken for granted to be purely physical, and something apart from spiritual wholeness. It therefore signifies, not the balanced staff, but only the physical end up, of the staff, and the location of consciousness in the body which will surely lead the finite ego to seek bodily pleasures. This tendency of consciousness will inevitably lead to pain, and the finite ego thus will see-saw from one end of the staff to the other until it maintains its position at the centre.

Accordingly consciousness located in the body, and giving a sense of physical lustiness, is, in reality, incompleteness and lack of Wholeness. While *pain,* which in itself is only the other end up, of the staff, is only a second woe, and consciousness still out of its true position. But the equilibrium of these two woes, finally enable consciousness to assume its equilibrium. They teach the way to true Health. Without the action of the woe of pleasure, and the reaction of the woe of pain, consciousness could never realize its celestial heritage. Herein is the *Worth of the two woes.* Pleasure is as much a disease as is pain. Pleasure and pain are head and foot of the staff of disease, and disease is the inverted reflection, or, contradictory of Health.

When I can invert Disease and read it from right to left, then I know the mystery of Health and not before. Pleasure and pain are a doublestrand twisted together into the reflected half of a word. This reflected half is, *either* Disease, or finite Health, but the other half, the contradictory of Disease, is the perfect *ease* of true Health, while WHOLENESS is the equilibrium between the refraction and reflection which cuts or distinguishes between the inseparable; for true cutting is uniting. It mysteriously combines the double strands which were twisted in opposite directions.

Thus this process of *healing* is the process of assimilating, and assimilating is *Reading* (rod-ing) — exoteric and esoteric reading, therefore *healing* is *reading*. Exoteric healing with minerals and drugs is only exoteric reading and an indispensable first step toward esoteric reading, or healing. I must learn the *symbols* of words before I can learn the *words*. But when I come to know that healing, reading and assimilating take place through IMAGES, then there is no longer need of communicating with external words. I can communicate directly through the Images. The Images communicate my thought without my going out to hunt up a clumsy drug or mineral to act as interpreter.

Again, with our lips we all speak foreign tongues to each other, but the Images speak the language of the heart; there is no misunderstanding them.

The Law of Contradictories is also the Law of communication as well as the Law of manifestation, for the object and purpose of *man-i-fest-ation* is communication. And if assimilating, reading and healing are all different degrees of communication, then must this Law of Contradictories be the Law of The Most High, mystically expressed as Yea, yea; Nay, nay, but which translated in terms of staff or proportion, reads

    1   2   3
yea : nay : : Yea : Nay. yea and nay *are* contradictory or reflected opposites of Yea and Nay the true and Polar Opposites.

The force with which the terrestrial fibres of pleasure and pain twist away from the celestial fibres they reflect (contradict), but express the force with which the two strands will enfold each other when the finite *will* removes the pressure with which it clings to its idols and turns toward the true ray, and toward its celestial *Source*.

Healing, — making whole, is therefore, the last and greatest Word for me to learn. It is the process of combining the contradictory parts of the drama into a magnificent *Whole*, and entering into the spirit of the Divine Author; It is a recalling of the parts I have been learning since the beginning of time. It is the assuming of the robes and characters I have been so long and painfully elaborating. And finally it is a swinging out from time into eternity to enact a part prepared for me from the beginning.

Looking out into this vast Universe I see only Mind in process of evolution. Each ray is a Thought-ray in development by means of refraction and reflection. Equilibrium, or Central-point, whenever it occurs, is Consciousness in process of realization. Motion is Reasoning in process of radiation. The Reasoning which is spiral and Spiritual.

LESSON XIV.

CONCLUSION— THE WALL.

Will implies Freedom. If I have no power of choice, then I, evidently, have no will of my own. Moreover, if I have no Freedom (implied by Will), then I am the most abject of slaves.

In the ancient ceremony of manumission the slave was touched with the rod, as a symbol of the fact that the ray frees from bonds of delusion.

Again in the rite of *Knighthood*, which admits to the privilege of bearing arms, the rod bore an important part.

Accordingly before I can enter upon my heritage, before I can seat myself upon my *Throne* and assume my Scepter, I must, first, be freed from slavery, and, second, I must be endowed with the privilege of bearing arms. But before I can receive a scepter and rule I must know how to rule, — before I can receive the honors of Knighthood I must know *how* to build a *Wall* and defend my possessions.

(1.) To know how to rule I must be able to balance the rod of *Justice* and *Mercy*. Now, Justice and Mercy are not Contradictories, as the world seems to have taken for granted, but they are Polar Opposites of the same rod. They mutually imply each other, and are simply unthinkable apart; for Justice without Mercy is not just; — for Mercy without Justice is blindly cruel, and therefore not Mercy at all.

Now the perfect equilibrium between Justice and Mercy is perfect power of choice, or *perfect Freedom*. For, since when I am ruled I am not *free*, if I am ever ruled in the slightest degree by my affections, then I am neither just nor merciful, and if my sense of Justice preponderates over my affection, then I am neither just nor merciful, and therefore am not free. It thus directly follows that I am not free, until I balance the rod of Justice and Mercy, and, moreover, since *Freedom* (power of choice) implies *Will*, it also directly follows that when I am free, then I shall know the meaning of Will, and not before.

Now, just as true *Freedom* is the exact contradictory of freedom on the finite plane, — so true *Will* is the exact contradictory of will on the finite plane. And since will implies freedom, my true *Will* is my emancipation from slavery, and it is also (as I have just seen) the power which confers the *right to rule*. My true Will, therefore, becomes my *Wall of Strength*, which I next consider how to build.

(2.) Our word *Wall* is from the Latin, as well as from Saxon, Dutch, etc. In the Saxon it is the same word as *weal, strength, soundness*, etc. The Latin vallus is a stake or post, and doubtless the wall originally was a palisade of posts. The primary sense of vallus is a shoot, suggesting at once *ray, ear,* etc. From this I also see at once hozv to build my wall. I must concentrate together rods as troops. All my forces, or possessions, I must con-centre, as converging lines or rays, so that they all meet at a common point.

And thus to build my wall of *Will* I must acquire the *Power of Concentration.*

But before I can do this, and in order to acquire the Power of Concentration, I must make the last and the greatest *oblation* of all. Before I can know the true Will I must offer up its contradictory. I must resign the finite will with all its finite desires, before I can know the True. But, manifestly, it is utter folly to make this offering before it is mine to make *i. e.,* before I am Free. And since to be free I must know how to balance the rod of Justice and Mercy, I turn once more to consider again this rod.

Freedom is the point of equilibrium between Justice and Mercy. Will is the power of *Concent-er-ing,* or of Ray-ing about the Centre, accordingly I discern the very *Highest Manifestation of the Quarterni.*

Head.   Foot.   Centre. Motion.

Justice: Mercy: Freedom: Will.

This proportion expresses the Quarterni of Ray evolved to its highest power. And when my soul realizes this perfect Harmony, then I am forever free from the illusions of birth and death. And *Will* is the Motive force which will propel, throughout Eternity, the perfectly balanced rod of Justice and Mercy.

Therefore this *Power of Concentering* is the last and greatest acquirement. Its attainment is the great *Weal;* its lack is the great *Woe.* To secure it is to realize WHOLENESS, to fail is *Chaos* and

Nothingness. And in order to attain this great *Weal* I must offer up the oblation of a true High Priest. And in order to secure the *Perfect Peace* of Wholeness I must fight the fight of the *True Warrior*. A Warrior capable of bearing and hurling a *lance*. I, therefore, turn to the *Staff* with which I started. This conclusion is, after all, only another beginning. The Ray of Light is now my *Lance* armed with which I continue my spiral and unending course in *Reality*.

APPENDIX.

OUTLINE LESSON IN OPTICS.

I. Refraction.

Rays of light in passing (Perpendicular rays pass directly through without being bent) obliquely from one medium to another are *bent* (refracted) from their course, — the degree of bending (refraction) rough without being bent, depending upon the *density*, or *rarity* of the medium.

Thus in passing into a medium of greater density (*e. g.,* from air to water), rays will be bent towards a perpendicular. But in passing from a denser to a rarer medium (*e. g.,* from water to air), they will be bent *from* a perpendicular towards a horizontal. (Insert illustration here)

(a.) Let A B represent a surface of water, then the perpendicular ray D C will pass to D E B (&.) But the oblique ray F C, instead of passing to F I will be bent at C and pass to F G, or *towards* the perpendicular.

(c.) The oblique ray G C in passing from water to air (from denser to rarer medium) will be bent at C and instead of passing to G H will be bent to G F, or *towards* the horizontal A B.

II. Reflection.

Rays of light falling obliquely upon a polished surface are thrown off in a new direction, and the angles of contact (incidence) and the angles of departure (reflection) are always equal.

Let A B represent a polished surface, then the perpendicular ray D C falling upon this surface will B be thrown directly back from C to D. But the oblique ray E C will be thrown off in the direction C F, and the *angle G will equal the angle H*.

The more nearly perpendicular the ray E C, the more nearly perpendicular will be the ray C F, — or again, the more nearly horizontal the ray E C, the more nearly horizontal will be the ray C F. Yet the angles H and G will always be equal; for the size of the angle H implies the size of the angle G, just as the direction of the ray E C implies the direction of the ray C F.

III. Relation of Refraction to Reflection.

All oblique rays of light, in passing into our atmosphere must be more or less bent before they reach reflecting surfaces, and must therefore, be *Refracted*, or *Incident* Rays before they can be *Reflected* Rays. And since *Reflected* rays and angles depend upon *Incident* rays and angles, it directly follows that the relation of *Refraction to Reflection* is that of *cause* to *effect*, of *action* to *reaction*, or in other words, Refraction and Reflection are polar opposites which mutually imply each other.

Every direct and true Refraction implies an inverted Reflection, and the existence of the one proves the existence of the other. Sight, Heat, Sound, Motion and *Thought* are all manifested through Refraction and Reflection.

Very Truly
T. H. Burgoyne.

Collaborator

Some of the most influential authors in 19th century esoteric circles were women writing about male adept heroes, for example Emma Hardinge Britten and Helena Petrovna Blavatsky. Often they used male alter egos to express claims that were actually reflections of their own experiences. "The adepts" were described in masculine terms, yet their greatest propagandists were women. In the case of *The Light of Egypt*, to the extent that she was Thomas H. Burgoyne's co-author, Grimké joined the ranks of female writers giving authorial credit to male adepts. This primary doctrinal book of the Hermetic Brotherhood of Luxor is as mysterious an example of pseudonyms as any book produced by Theosophists, Rosicrucians, or Spiritualists. Burgoyne, the most prolific author associated with the Hermetic Brotherhood of Luxor, was its secretary for several years after its founding in 1884. Born in Douglas, Isle of Man, in 1855 as Thomas Henry Dalton, he was living in Bradford, Yorkshire as of the 1881 census which found him married to Betsy Bella Prince and father of two children. His earliest known correspondence with Brotherhood members was from Burnley, Lancashire in early 1886, but by May of that year he had relocated to White County, Georgia, with the family of HBL co-founder Peter Davidson, having left his own family in England. Establishing an HBL colony in America was a failed venture, but the Davidson family successfully established themselves in their new community. Burgoyne continued his journey westward and within a year had arrived in California where he began a collaboration with Grimké.

The name T.H. Burgoyne was a pseudonym adopted around the time the HBL was founded in 1884. But within a short time it was revealed that his real name was Thomas Henry Dalton (sometimes d'Alton), and that he had served six months in prison in England in 1883 for advertising fraud. This news was spread broadcast by Theosophists who saw it as a way to discredit a rival organization. The ensuing controversy destroyed the HBL in England, but not in France where it continued to thrive, nor in

America where Dalton arrived as Burgoyne with Peter Davidson and family in 1886.[122]   Burgoyne had been using Zanoni as a pen name ever since the first issue of *The Occultist* was published in England in 1885. *Zanoni* was a Rosicrucian themed 1842 novel by Edward Bulwer-Lytton, in which the adept teacher of the title character was named Mejnour. Peter Davidson, Provincial Grand Master of the North of the original HBL, wrote under the latter pen name. Zanoni's identity was so well concealed that Emma Hardinge Britten was twice accused by Theosophists of authoring *The Light of Egypt*. In response, Britten heaped praise on Burgoyne and scorn on his attackers, and later wrote a glowing review of his book.[123]

Why would former close associates of Emma Hardinge Britten presume her to be the author? *The Light of Egypt* continues the occult mythos and doctrines of *Art Magic* and *Ghost Land* more than do any of Britten's own later Spiritualist books. It is also more in line with *Isis Unveiled* than are any of Blavatsky's later Theosophical books. Burgoyne's Zanoni positions himself as successor to *Ghost Land*'s Chevalier Louis, with Britten's encouragement and support, in a chain of neo-Hermetic adepts. The 289 page edition of 1889 was succeeded by a 1900 edition, which included an additional 174 page Volume II. Returning after many years to add a second volume in a more mature voice is a parallel feature of Burgoyne's Zanoni and Britten's Louis.

Burgoyne first traveled to California in 1887, after time in Georgia with Peter Davidson's family, in Topeka, Kansas with HBL member W.W. Allen, and in Denver with what was becoming the largest local group of Brotherhood members. (See *Letters to the Sage*, Volume 1, for data on the membership of the HBL.) Meanwhile, in early 1887 Sarah sent her daughter Angelina to live in Hyde Park with her father, after which she appears to have spent at least the next year in California. The precise contribution of Grimké to *The Light of Egypt* was later described by Elbert Benjamine as assisting with The Science of the Stars portion of the 1889 edition. It seems the work of a more disciplined and better educated writer than the preceding Science of the Soul portions, which echo

Burgoyne's earlier periodical writings, influenced by the examples of Britten's *Art Magic* and *Ghost Land*.

Like *Ghost Land, Isis Unveiled,* and other works of the period, the contested authorship of *The Light of Egypt* invites the reader to distinguish among authorial voices. Book II of the 1900 edition is explained as Burgoyne's "posthumous contribution" which was "dictated by the author from the subjective plane of life (to which he ascended several years ago) through the laws of mental transfer, well known to all occultists..."[124] Burgoyne's Zanoni is a male echoing a succession of female authors, thus a mirror image of Britten and Blavatsky's adepts and Masters. One of the most salient echoes of Chevalier Louis is Zanoni's claim to have made "personal investigations, extending over a series of years in England, France, Germany, Austria, and the United States, with various types and phases of mediums.[125]" In *The Key to Theosophy,* Blavatsky complained, with ample justification, of the continuity of adepts "used as sledge-hammers to break the theosophical heads with" which "began twelve years ago, with Mrs. Emma Hardinge Britten's `Louis' of *Art Magic* and *Ghost-Land,* and now ends with the `Adept' and `Author' of *The Light of Egypt.*"[126]

The writings of Sarah's final decade reflect collaboration with Burgoyne, but the place, time, and circumstances of their association are unknown. A possible clue about her travels written during her lifetime is a letter dated 29 December 1890, in which the Reverend W.A. Ayton wrote from Chacombe Vicarage to Francis G. Irwin:

We knew the whole history of Burgoyne, and that he had been a curse to every one who employed him, a thorough deep-dyed scoundrel. We know all about him since he has been in America. He left a wife and family in England, but has married again there. The last I heard was that if he sees 2 or 3 men in the distance approaching his quarters he turns pale and trembles. It is supposed he has been guilty of something which puts him in mortal fear, and that he contemplates going off to Australia.[127]

Sarah was posthumously revealed to have lived in the Antipodes in the early 1890s, but not in Australia. More than ten years passed before Archibald and Angelina received any further news of Sarah. Her death in California was reported to them from Hartford, in a letter dated October 1, 1898, written by Emma Austin Tolles to Angelina.

> I am very sorry to be the bearer of sad news though Mrs. Stuart may have told you, for she has been informed of your dear mother's passing on to higher planes...She never ceased to love you as dearly as ever and it was a great trial to her to have you go away from her, how great God alone knows, but it was the only thing to do...She had every thing done that could be done, she wrote me just as long as she could make a mark but finally grew so weak she could not hold a pencil. The nurse says she wanted her watch sent to you and there may be some thing else- they will send it probably to Mrs. Stuart and she will give it to you.[128]

However, when Tolles praises Sarah as a distinguished author, she refers not to Mrs. Stuart's teachings but to *The Light of Egypt*:

> Your mother, dear Angelina was one of the most wonderful souls that ever came to this planet. When you are old enough to understand I will tell you about her wonderful career. This world has been a scorching fire through which she has passed and now she has gone to a reward that few of us can conceive of—Her book "the Light of Egypt" is the most wonderful book of modern times though she says it will be one hundred years before the world will recognize it—She nearly lost her life in writing it but her soul never flinched from a duty. She had two or three friends who have stood by

her from first to last, who have considered it a privilege to do so.[129]

Just over a month passed before Moses Stanley wrote to Butler Wilson about complications involving Sarah's estate. The correspondence seems to imply that neither he nor anyone in the family had yet contacted Archibald directly, and that Sarah had sworn them to secrecy in the matter of her whereabouts, known to Tolles, Stuart, and the Wagners and to her Stanley relatives but concealed from her husband and daughter. Stanley addressed Wilson as the attorney for Mr. Grimké, asking him to consult with the bereaved husband on Sarah's estate, which consisted of $529 in the Hibernian Trust and Loan Society of San Francisco. "When she realized that she must die she sent her Bank Book to Dr. Wagner her publisher & friend, evidently desiring him to pay her debts and forward the balance to Nana, and so also we instructed him."[130] Archibald's response must have been encouraging of further confidences, as on November 16, 1898, Moses replied to him:

> Sarah's action in regard to the money is to me perfectly unaccountable. When she left for New Zealand, she deposited in the British Columbia Bank of San Francisco $1000 sending me the duplicate draft, with orders, if she died, to draw the money and pay it to Nana. She knew she was liable to sudden death at any moment. On the street, in Auckland N.Z. near the Post Office, she had a heart failure, and fell. The physician brought her to, and she decided to return home; but he told her she would never live to reach America with such a heart – she surely would be buried in the ocean. But she reached home, and was with us a year and a half and went to San Diego to die of poison.
>
> It was her wish that Dr. Wagner should draw the money – pay her bills and forward the balance to Nana, but sent no check with the Bank Book.

Dr. Wagner is a Physician, Publisher, and literary man. He published her book on Oriental Philosophy – a book of some 400 pages, which has been through six Editions and some pamphlets – and with the Bank Book she enclosed an unfinished story.[131]

Stanley asked for the cooperation of Archibald Grimké in resolving the need for an estate administrator in California, as Henry Wagner had "relinquished all idea of having anything to do with the money business when he sent the Bank Book to Mrs. Tolles for Nana."[132] The last letter that Archibald received from Moses about his late wife's demise was written in Detroit on February 18, 1899. The bereaved father wrote "I did not tell you, I could not – of the last sad scene of her earthly life - a scene that forever hallows the waves of San Diego Bay. By her request, her friends, at the setting of the sun, gathered on the shores, and a few went out in a boat, carrying the urn that contained her ashes, and scattered them over the limpid waves. So there is not now a vestige of our dearly beloved one remaining."[133] He told Archibald that her letters were usually signed Sarah, sometimes S.E. Stanley, and enclosed one written in Auckland, New Zealand, in which Sarah lamented that "O if I only had Nana with me how much happier I should be."[134]

Angelina Weld Grimké

Angelina's last communication about her mother's writings from Emma Austin Tolles came on January 3, 1900, a date that inspired enthusiasm about the new century:

> My dear Angelina: How queer it seems to write 1900! --- 1881 closed the Cycle and we entered upon a new one, the most important and momentous of our Race- It will last about 2000- years then the 5th race- will begin to go down... It is only natural that you should write for your mother and Father are both talented in that direction—Do you write on the impulse, spontaneously or by deliberate applied effort? Do you get impressions as you used to get them? There was a time when you first came to me that you used to <u>see</u> and <u>hear</u> clairvoyantly and clairaudiently?[135]

A trace of the Christian Science origins of the Stuart group can be found in the reservations Tolles expresses about material medicine:

> I am glad you like your school and studies- I think it an excellent training—and very beneficial to health. I do not think much of the Medical Profession—M D's as a profession studying into matter, body, which is the effect, ignoring mind and Soul where <u>causation</u> lies. The human body is a wonderful beautiful instrument, and it is an instrument, that is just what it was intended for the Soul is or should be the operation which this instrument under complete control.[136]

One of Angelina's earliest literary works is a poignant expression of grief at the loss of her mother; Sarah's death being only the final confirmation of a loss that occurred when Angelina was put on a cross country train by herself at the age of seven. In the *Selected Works of Angelina Weld Grimké*, the story "Black is as Black Does: a Dream" is classified as fiction, but to the reader familiar with her family history the "story" does not read as fiction.

Published in the *Colored American Magazine* in August 1900, it seems to reflect the encouragement from Emma Austin Tolles earlier that year for Angelina to engage in writing that was impulsive, spontaneous, and perhaps clairaudient and clairvoyant. It is her encounter with Sarah on the other side:

> It came to me one, dark, rainy, morning. I was half awake and half asleep. The wind was blowing drearily, and I listened to the swish of the rain on the glass, and the dripping from the eaves and as I lay listening, I thought many things and my thoughts grew hazier and hazier until I fell into deep slumber.

Then, methought, a great feeling of peace come upon me, and that all my cares were falling from me and rolling away— away into infinity. So I lay with my eyes closed and this great feeling of peace increased and my heart was glad within me. Then some one touched me lightly on the shoulder and eyes, and my heart gave a great bound, for I was not prepared for the loveliness of the scene, that now burst upon my sight. All around stretched a wide, green, grassy, plain. Each little blade of grass sang in the gentle wind, and here and there massive trees spread their branches, and the leaves sang, and the birds, and a river that passed through the meadow sparkled and sang as it sped on its way. And listening, I heard no discord, for all the voices flowed into each other, and mingled, and swelled and made one, grand, sweet, song. I longed to sing too, and lifted up my voice, but no song came so that I wondered. And a voice at my side, answered, "Thou art not one of us yet." And the voice was sweeter than the babbling brook, tenderer than the voice of a mother to her erring child, lower than the beating of the surf upon the short. Then I turned to see whence the voice came, and as I looked I fell weeping on my face.

For there stood before me a figure clad in white, and as she moved she seemed like a snowy cloud, that sails over the sky in the summer-time, and a soft light shone above, around, behind, illuminating her, but it was not for this that I fell weeping. I had looked upon the face, and the truth that shone forth from the mild eyes, the sweetness that smiled around the mouth, and all the pity, the mercy, the kindness expressed in that divine countenance revealed to me how wicked I was and had been. But she took me by the hand, bidding me arise, and kissing me on the brow. And between my sobs I asked, "Where am I?" and the low voice answered, "This is heaven," and I said, "Who art thou?" and she answered "One of the lovers of God." And as she she spoke that name, the heavens brightened, the grass sang sweeter, and the leaves and the birds and the silvery river, and looking up I saw that she was no longer by my side, but was moving over the plain, and turning she beckoned to me. And I followed. [137]

As Angelina's experiences of the afterlife continue, she reveals herself as her father's daughter and introduces the theme of racial injustice that will dominate her drama, fiction, and nonfiction in the new century. She witnesses a black murder victim being made whole and sent heavenwards, after which his white murderer is condemned to hell. "I saw that his skin was white but his soul was black. For it makes a difference in Heaven whether a man's *soul* be black or white!"[138] This suggests that her visionary encounter with Sarah reveals the literary legacy of both parents; the introspective style of her poetry and fiction shows traces of Sarah, but the political subject matter of her nonfiction and drama is invariably a continuation of the Grimké-Weld family heritage on both sides of the color line. In her 2016 study *Aphrodite's Daughters*, poetry scholar Maureen Honey comments that the effect of her mother's abandonment was apparent in the way Angelina "not only obsessively returns to moments of longing, regret, and sadness in her poetry" but that "her speakers also commune directly with the dead through transcendental mergers with the natural world."[139] This recurring theme appears in her earliest childhood verses, prompting Honey to comment that "For a young girl to meditate on death in such a lyrical, even romantic, way suggests deep wells of grief and loss soothed by the imagined embrace of lost dear ones in an unseen celestial sphere free of pain"[140] adding that "These efforts to maintain a loving relationship with her daughter clearly meant something to the seven-year-old Nana, for she kept these letters the rest of her life and they repeatedly express the idea that separated loved ones could fashion an enduring bond in a spiritual realm."[141]

Zanoni After Sarah

In 2019 I made three presentations of evidence concerning Sarah's collaborator known as Burgoyne, first at the biennial Church of Light conference in New Mexico in June, then in absentia at the International Theosophical History Conference in Athens, Greece in October, and finally at the Thomas Moore Johnson centennial symposium at Missouri State University in November as a report on ongoing investigations. Those inquiries are now focused on his life in the twentieth century but have already yielded results about the 1890s that reveal what became of Zanoni after Sarah left for New Zealand in the late 1880s.

Before collaborating with Sarah on *The Light of Egypt*, Burgoyne had used the pseudonym Zanoni for periodical articles while Peter Davidson used that of another character from the same novel, Mejnour. After Sarah's departure from the United States, Zanoni continued as author of two more books despite Burgoyne vanishing from the scene after 1891. The Thomas Moore Johnson correspondence provides many letters and documents from Burgoyne, which helped to shed light on the development of the Hermetic Brotherhood of Luxor in the US. By comparison with another set of letters that emerged in 2016 in western North Carolina, we can now celebrate real progress in solving the mysteries surrounding Burgoyne's later life under a new name.

A parish birth register in the Johnson correspondence provides the date and place of his birth and the names of his parents. Son of chiropodist Thomas Henry D'Alton and his wife

Emma Rice D'Alton, he was born April 14, 1855 in Douglas, Isle of Man. Thomas Henry Burgoyne's birth chart with the date of April 14, 1855 and coordinates (rounded off to whole numbers) in the Irish Sea near the Isle of Man appears in Volume One of the Brotherhood of Light books, *Laws of Occultism*.

Although Burgoyne's three known mentor figures were remarkably diverse in ethnic and religious backgrounds, they were misidentified with one another as hopeless confusion reigns in published sources about the identity and pseudonyms of the original Hermetic Brotherhood of Luxor leaders. This confusion extended to Burgoyne and all his mentors and hence to *The Light of Egypt*. Furthermore, Britten's literary alliance with Burgoyne is clearly evident in her comments on his books, and they are likely to have met in England before his departure in 1886, but no evidence to that effect has yet emerged, adding another layer of confusion.

In the summer of 1891 an announcement appeared for a forthcoming book to be sold by Thomas H. Burgoyne in Mendocino County, California. The proposed *Celestial Dynamics* was not in fact published until 1896, as authored by Zanoni. But Zanoni had by then emerged as an astrology teacher in the first book published by Astro-Philosophical Publications of Denver, *Language of the Stars* in 1892; the name Burgoyne was abandoned for both these tomes. In the same year Norman Astley married "Theresa Thompson" in Boston. Their marriage document conflicts in multiple ways with other documents about the two partners. Overwhelming evidence shows that Burgoyne had taken the identity of Astley when marrying Stebbins and continued to live under this identity through their forty-year marriage and beyond. Stebbins had disguised her first name when marrying Astley in Boston, but her surname was indeed Thompson at the time.

Genevieve Stebbins had married Joseph Thompson in 1888 and was partnered with his sister Mary in her New York business, which attracted such clients as Mrs. Pierpont Morgan and Mrs. John D. Rockefeller. The only evidence of a connection between Burgoyne and Stebbins in the 1880s is his recommending her writings in his private lessons to his pupils, undated letters quoted in a 1963 edition of *The Light of Egypt*. Astley's role as a collaborator in Stebbins's school is evident in their 1893 copyrights for a pantomime entitled *The Myth of Isis*, along with the related *The Myth of Ariadne*.

Joint acquisition of property in the mountains of North Carolina began about the time of the marriage of the Astleys and lasted a dozen years until they retired to England. Norman's life managing remote properties in Burke County was far removed from the social life of Blowing Rock with Genevieve; he resided in a rustic cabin rather than the "pretty cottage" he described as inhabiting with her in the town. Handwriting of Norman Astley has recently emerged from a Burke County local historian whose ancestors owned land formerly owned by the Astleys, where she now resides and has inherited Astley letters that can be compared with the Burgoyne letters in Missouri. Neil Cantwell is trained in forensic document analysis and concludes on the basis of abundant written evidence that Astley's handwriting is identical to Burgoyne's in many definitive ways, from individual letters to common words like the or and, and especially signatures. Further light on Astley is provided by *The Quest of the Spirit*, published by 1913 by Stebbins as editor and A Pilgrim of the Way as author.[142]

Astley's first emergence in print in England was a letter to the British Empire Naturalist Association in December 1908, in which he enthuses about local wildlife just as he had in his North Carolina letters of the previous decade. He is living in Devon, and relocated to Guernsey, Sussex and California with Genevieve, before finally returning to Devon after her death with his third wife Nellie. In 1939 as a widower yet again in Plymouth Norman gave his date of birth for the census as April 14, 1855, the same date as in the D'Alton birth register and the natal chart of Burgoyne.

A TOUR THROUGH THE ZODIAC

SEQUEL TO

First Lessons In Reality

LESSON I.

THE WARRIOR.

As a slave, in bondage to sense and seeming, with a simple staff in my hand, I started out in my first studies in search for the Pole-Star of truth — for truth implies freedom.

But now I commence the second round of my spiral ladder as a warrior, armed with a lance, for I have learned that I must be able to defend my possessions and acquisitions in truth before I can obtain a scepter and rule.

Now a scepter has two ends; a head, or master, who wields it, and a foot, or slave, who is *"under the rod;"* and, since these two ends cannot be detached, the ruler and the serf are the two halves of a unit, while at this point of unity is the true King.

So, in my own individual case, at the same time that I am a slave I am also a master. I comprise the two within my system. If I have been a slave of some, I must also have been a tyrant to others.[143]

Therefore, since the King alone is free, before I can realize freedom I must be able to maintain the point of equilibrium between the tyrant and the slave, and it will, most assuredly, be an incessant warfare until this harmony is experienced. The true warrior must combine into a unity the slave of sense, or sensualist, on the one hand, with the tyrant, who would ignore and destroy sense, on the other.

But I wish, in entering upon so formidable an undertaking, for a fixed point from whence to start. I must have a center in order to describe a circumference; yet, since the point of equilibrium is just the thing for which I am about to engage in warfare, I hesitate no longer, but at once rush forward into the melee of shadows, with my lance poised ready to hurl. But lo! my lance, poised in my hand, turns my ray-of-light — my clew-of-thread, and the shadows are already breaking before the mystic point of this lance. Having hurled it, I watch it revolve as it speeds on its course, and at its mystic point, where it strikes and refracts, I behold the bow of promise — the beautiful seven-point-star. This star is the point I seek, the mystic point of radiation, of equilibrium, of harmony. Its seven colors, blending through infinite tints and shades into the pure white light, are the seven-fold mysteries of Unity in Infinity, the Unity-in-Infinity which is the mystery of Godliness.

In my "First Studies of Reality" this seven-point-star at once divided itself (the first and last, however, being in reality one, or the mystic Thirteen) into polar-opposites, or chromatics of fourteen lessons, just as each of the seven colors has its complementary ray, which is invisible to exoteric vision, the esoteric quality of which may be expressed by the esoteric terms written over each color. (See diagram of seven-point-star.)[p64]

Starting with red, the zenith of the figure, and the color least refracted from the celestial white, I observe that the figure outlined by the point in the circumference, the lines, staff and wall, the dotted lines, and the point at the center is a diamond, the hardest, or most fixed, substance known; and well does the diamond symbolize my throne and point-of-equilibrium. And, surely, only the highest wisdom can ever enable me to attain this balance, and all wisdom truly begins and ends with it. It is Alpha and Omega.

The visible red is symbolic of blood, sensuality, suffering and ignorance. Therefore, following the Law of Contradictories, the invisible red expresses the blood turned to wine, sensuality to spirituality, suffering to power, ignorance to the most unspeakable wisdom. But how marvelously is this spiritual-ray hidden from the worldly-wise and prudent; for, just as red is the color those afflicted with color-blindness cannot discern, so the invisible red is just the wisdom hidden from those who are spiritually color-blind.

The form of motion by which the white ray breaks out into the seven colors is the first, from center to circumference, but the form which concenters, and to realize which I am about to engage in warfare, is the second — the exact reverse of the first. Therefore, as in the "First Lessons in Reality" my studies outlined, or circumscribed, the seven-point-star, so now I pass from circumference to center, and accordingly reverse my diagram; i. e., turn my seven-point-star outside in. First I reverse the cardinal points, turning the right hand to the left; east becomes west and north becomes south. Red, the least refracted ray, is the beginning and end of the point at the center. Next orange, rising in the east, the union of visible and audible, forms its point at the center, or throne, and so on round the circle until the seven color-points blend into a unity at the foot of my throne, from thence to ray forth on a higher plane and in larger spirals.

Although this second round of my ladder, as a whole, follows the second form of motion, yet each day's march of this expedition must follow the first line of motion, while each night my forces indraw to the camp-fire at the center. Day is the raying out of the seven points to the circumference; night the raying back to the one-point center.

Only I must not here lose myself in these symbols. The Seven-fold Morning Star is the Temple of the Body; the reversed Evening Star is the Holy of Holies, wherein the soul meets the Most High. But Lucifer and Venus are one star, not two; as formerly supposed.

Therefore I am about to engage in warfare, to establish the true and only harmony between soul and body. This physical temple, neglected or in ruins, must be rebuilt and re-occupied before the soul can meet its God. This is the only way under the Sun whereby men can be saved. This is the Corner-Stone, so long rejected by all our builders.[144] Physical health and truth — the truth which is above, beneath and roundabout all religions, mutually imply each other, and are absolutely unthinkable apart.

Body, this inverted and left-sided reflection of soul, is the only trysting-place between the soul and its Divine source. Therefore, as a warrior and worshiper I seek the diamond-point of wisdom, where the red-ray blends into its spiritual counterpart.

LESSON II.

THE FIERY TRIPLICITY.

♈, OR WATCHING.

On my first round of this spiral ladder I proceeded by quadrants, or the quarterni, as expressed in the terms ray-ment, food, house and hearth-fire. But, on this second round, my advance follows according to triplicities, or the four equilateral triangles. (See diagram.)[p64]

Taken by twos, and placed side by side, they form two diamonds; on being interlaced, they comprehend all the mysteries.

The quadrant is a fourth part of the Zodiac, containing three consecutive signs. A triplicity is a fourth part of the Zodiac, containing three signs, each of which are four signs apart. Thus, the first triplicity, starting with ♈ (symbol-for head and face, and exalted above all as containing eyes) will be the equilateral triangle, having its vertices at the signs (Aries, Leo, Sagittarius), or the Lessons Visible, Eating and Hearth.

In proceeding by quadrants, the four great Kingdoms, Earth, Fire, Water and Air (motion), were regarded separately, yet I found the first three were only modes of ray-ing, or motion, and that they all interpenetrate and balance from one to the other. Just so now, although fire zeal, courage, etc., are the first requisites in a good warrior, which he must have on all occasions; yet this Fiery Triplicity expresses the more active forms of fire, whereas it is, as it were, only latent in the other triplicities.

Turning to the diagram of the seven-point-star, ♈, or visible, is the red ray, which, together with the yellow ray of audible, ♉, unite to form orange. Therefore the red ray is one side of my equilateral triangle; next ♌, or eating, is the yellow ray in the formation of green, so yellow is another side of the triangle, while the third side is from ♐ hearth, the blue ray in the formation of indigo. Accordingly, the Fiery Triplicity has for its three sides the three primary colors, red, yellow and blue. Thus the primary chord in color, or in sound, also expresses the primary element of fire. And this is true of all the other triplicities as well as the fiery. Thus:

	{Audible.	Assimilating.	Ray.
Earthy.	♉	♍	♑
	{Yellow.	Blue.	Red.

	{Hunger.	Door.	Law.
Watery.	♋	♏	♓
	{Yellow.	Blue.	Red.

	{Tangible.	Proportion.	Images.
Airy	♊	♎	♒
	{Yellow.	Blue.	Red.

It is the red ray in (Aquarius) which is used both in the formation of indigo and violet, its chemical property; whereas the red, or key, note C of the scale is the Heat-ray. This is the mystery of the octave. The key note C is the red of heat, but, refracted in its spiral course through the scale, it circles round and reaches its starting place one octave higher.

On this higher plane, after having been blent with the yellow of trial and temptation and the blue of knowledge, it expresses the mystic, magnetic, electric melody of the seventh, whether in color, sound or soul.

In this formation of the triplicities through the primary chords is expressed a most profound mystery, and upon my ability to grasp this mystery depends my success as a warrior.

In entering upon the fiery ordeal I have to learn three lessons, correspondencies, or correlations of the three lessons: Visible, Eating and Hearth.

The first implies the Warrior Seeing, or as a Sentinel, Watching.

The second implies the Warrior Acting, or Sacrificing.

The third lesson is the Warrior judging from the results of the sacrifices, or, to use the mystic terms of the ancients, "*discerning the omens from inspecting the entrails of the victims offered at sacrifice.*" [145]

So, now, as the warrior detailed to my first duty, I climb my watch-tower to watch (as the ancients said) for the "flights of birds;" i. e., I must see the esoteric reality in the exoteric shadow phantoms.

My eyes must be trained to detect these "birds" from afar, either singly, as dots, or in companies of lines and curves. I must observe the direction of their flights and, from the law of motion, see first in my mind's eye the esoteric meaning of everything within the ken of my watch-tower, even while my physical eyes see only the powers of darkness draw with the eyes of soul, through the spirit-red-ray, I must to some extent have so conformed my life to truth as to have actually and consciously realized the Real from the Unreal. I must see that Body, Pleasure, Pain, Disease and Death are all illusions; that finite personalities, with their loves, hates, greeds and jealousies, are all illusions. Still further, I must see that each of these illusions, singly, is reflected over and over again, in every direction, so that the army drawn up against me, apparently so vast, is simply a reduplication of a few primary illusions.

I therefore give my attention to the primary illusions, for when they are dispelled the enemy is routed:

1 — The illusion of Body.

2 — The illusion of One's Self, refracted on the seven different planes.

3 — The illusions of Finite Self.

4 — The illusion that the Soul, or True Self, could ever be projected outside of the One Infinite Mind into Body, or Phenomena.

But when I can climb still higher in my tower, and can know there is no such thing as illusion; that truth is all there is; that One Mind and Father has made all there is, and that illusion and self never could be projected into Nothing outside of the All, then the sentinel has completed the watch.[146]

Yet, before I can climb to this height all the illusive phantom-self of personality must be burned or sacrificed (Leo) upon the altar of Heart ⟨↗⟩; i. e., I cannot rightly or truly see until after the other sides of my triplicity are filled in, for an equilateral triangle is not an equilateral triangle until it has three equal sides.

Just as from simply seeing flames with the physical eye I do not comprehend how they will affect my hand until I throw it into them, so, now, I cannot see until after the sacrifice unless I have first seen. So, in order to balance these contradictories, I now proceed to the sacrifice.

LESSON III.

THE FIERY TRIPLICITY.

♈ ♌ ♐

♌, OR SACRIFICING.

Fire is the great purifier. So action is that form of the Fiery Triplicity (yellow-ray side) which is the great purifier.

According to the former analysis, all action is sacrifice, passion and oblation, and it is through this trial by fire, and the sacrifice and suffering implied in it, that I gain my spiritual sight (insight) . And it is a delusion that my eyes can ever be opened to the nature of fire, except by experiencing it; for how can I ever know that illusion is illusion unless I experience its nothingness?

I may stand up before the enemy and repeat the words: "There is only one Mind; there is no illusion of finite personality," but, as far as vain repetition goes, I would better take some other creed, for herein is a great mystery. This awful law of contradictories works (when actually evoked) in spite of my unbelief, and even when I, in my blindness, do not see the results. This is the true creed of the Knowledge of Good and Evil and of the Tree of Life; and to partake of the fruit of this tree, tempted by the serpent of the lower nature, or self-mask, is to surely die.

If the lower self stumbles upon this true creed, or is entrusted with it unpurified by the trial of fire and suffering, the lie of personality is only accentuated. The mask thinks it has become as the Gods, and its fall is inevitable. It has taken exactly the opposite road for truth, and instead of realizing its oneness with the Divine Spirit it will fall to the very depths of the shadows of nothingness, even while mumbling the true creed.[147]

Yet this seeming and so-called fall is but the first form of action, without which there could be no reaction, and inaction is as fatal to insight as personality, accentuated to nothingness.

Since, in order to rise, there must be a seeming fall, so, in order to realize there is no such thing as illusion, I accept it as an hypothesis to get rid of it, just as it is necessary to demonstrate certain propositions in geometry to be untrue by assuming them to be true, for thus only can their untruth become self-evident; and in order to realize the Infinite One I am forced to postulate the finite personalities. And yet I also know that to even momentarily accept illusion chains me to it (for the time being) ; for I am where I locate myself, as One with the All, or as seemingly projected outside the All, where, like a soap-bubble, I shall speedily realize the lie of self-mask; the harder I blow this bubble the quicker it bursts into nothingness. Like a child, I can keep on blowing personality bubbles, only to see these finite Egos burst, one after another; or I can put away the childish things, resolving to be no longer deceived by them, and blow them only to understand the law according to which they come and go. Therefore I accept finite personalities solely to demonstrate their utter impossibility, and when I know that time is also an illusion, I rise to the plane where even the Sun itself will stand silent upon Gibeon, and the Moon stay in the valley of Ajalon until I avenge myself upon all my enemies.

Hereafter let me act, or refrain from acting, simply to know truth, and no longer conform to finite and worldly codes of morality or mere social traditions and usages.

Just as in a former lesson I accepted the visible Universe in its unity and in its infinity as a grand universal language, its sentences, letters and punctuation marks all symbols for thought and traced with the finger of God, so now I accept all terrestrial action as purely symbolic action, possessing no moral quality in itself, but simply descriptive of spiritual acts, which I cannot possibly comprehend until I have faithfully performed all the symbolic acts To refrain from these symbolic acts before I grasp the real acts is to deliberately bar and bolt the only door by which I can enter the temple, expecting thus to gain admittance. To refrain from flesh eating, from wine drinking and from social and family life, simply for the sake of abstinence, is to play the part of a stupid tyrant and not of the King. On the other hand, to debauch myself in all these acts, simply because they satisfy my senses, is to become the slave of suffering and death.

The mob must not rule, yet the tyrant who devastates his kingdom and puts all the inhabitants to death by fire, torture, or slow starvation, ends by having no kingdom to rule. If I destroy the mob because I fear it, I do not overcome fear by the process nor obtain wisdom.

I therefore sacrifice to idols, or shadowy images, simply to eliminate melody out of discord, to realize the "Octave of Purification," whereby the fire, which on the lower plane is destructive to life, is raised from the key-note C to the chemical, life-giving C of the scale.

From out this fiery furnace of trial this right action, knowledge and wisdom are born. The Christ-Truth must be born of this Tribe of the Lion (si). It can only come from this Royal Action, and is itself the highest and supreme sacrifice, whereby the Son of Man becomes the Son of God.

But I can never comprehend this last sacrifice until I have learned the meaning of all the other sacrifices, and how to make them. I must learn the meaning of eating, whereby the plant life and animal life are sacrificed, before I can comprehend the awful mystery of the sacrifice of human life, called death, even up to that sublime death on the Cross.

But sacrificing is not destroying, and to comprehend the meaning of eating, or sacrificing, or action, is to realize the absolute unthinkability of the illusion called death. Therefore, let me never take a morsel of food into my mouth without reflecting that I am performing the ceremonials of sacrifice within the temple of my body, just as the rites of public temple worship were formerly observed.

And let me study the meanings of all the correspondencies of these temple rites.

And, also, let me engage in all the acts of finite life; of trade, politics and social life, etc., until I learn the reality which makes the shadow, and thus burn every idol upon the altar of truth.

LESSON IV.

THE FIERY TRIPLICITY.

♈ ♌ ♐

♐, OR JUDGING.

As the victims have been slaughtered and consumed by the flames, the warrior must carefully collect together the ashes, or remnants, into the Sacred Urn of Pure-Heart, and then, placing them before the bar of conscience, await the responses.

These responses are judgments, proceeding from the Divinity within. If the offerings have been good and acceptable, and the rites properly observed, then the replies will surely be auspicious. But if the two former duties have not been properly performed, then am I guilty of the most awful sacrilege in approaching the Divinity profanely.

According to my own actions am I judged; my own conscience is the arbiter. This judge must give the decisions according to the manner in which the sentinel and the sacrificial priest have performed their tasks, for the judgment follows as inevitably as when, having placed two sides of an equilateral triangle together at the proper angle, the third side is the response, depending upon the other two.

Again, this response is the third note in the primary chord. If I have struck the first two, there is only one other which possibly can complete the chord.

Again, this response is the conclusion, or third term, in the perfect syllogism. The sentinel upon the watch-tower, having properly performed his duty, states the major premise; the sacrifice, with its implied suffering, gives out the minor note or premise; the Oracle speaks out the conclusion. Although the conclusion of a syllogism is its third term, yet it expresses the mystery of the trinity, for it is a trinity, and at the same time an organic unity. It combines the major and minor premises into a higher unity, which differs from either of them, just as the molecule of water combines two dissimilar elements into a unity differing from its component parts, and also as H and O combine with a lightning flash of soul which accompanies the combining together of the two premises of a syllogism into their higher unity, and is an intuitive spark from the altar of Divinity.

This altar is my Hearth ⬈ of Pure- Heart. Unless this Urn is sufficiently purified by properly accepting (not rejecting) the experiences of life, it cannot receive the ashes of the sacrifice and impart to them the Divine Spark which makes them over into a living, organic unity, on a higher plane than they were before, nor raise in power and might the ashes of actions sown in weakness and watered with tears of suffering. This expresses the mystery of the re-birth, whereby the physical body is raised to the plane of spiritual body while yet in the possession of the physical.

This is that which constitutes the spiritual plane upon which one is born. There is a Divine correspondence, and the latent possibilities of the soul have the corresponding possibilities in the brain, which can be brought forth to usefulness while in the physical body. Bringing about the harmony between the two constitutes re-birth.

There is only one way of being re-born, just as there is only one way to be born into the physical, and this one way is revealed through the fiery syllogism (triplicity), the major premise of which is Truth

Realized from the Sentry's Watch-tower, the minor premise of which is Love Actualized by the Sacrifice of Burnt Offerings, the conclusion of which is Life Immortalized, or lifted from the plane of Time to Eternity. This conclusion is the Immaculate Conception of the re-birth, which is conscious son-ship with the Father.

Truth realized frees from every illusion of sense and casts out every error and all diseases. Truth realized is liberty, for from or by the power born of Knowledge you can be free.

Love actualized, or practiced, recognizes the Divine origin of every soul, and that every form of life and condition is necessary to the unfoldment of the soul in its evolutionary steps of progress, and, comprehending the law of contradictories, knows only universal charity and communion of saints, those who have passed through the fires of purification and learned the lessons therein taught, without prejudice, sentiment or pain. Love actualized is Fraternity. Then are we able to look upon all life as one Divine Whole, recognizing all as one fraternity, each filling the necessary notes in the Anthem of Creative Life.

Life eternalized, making every moment eternity, lifts the soul to a plane above illusion. Realizing the realities of life leaves no room for illusions where, grasping the equality of ratios, it knows only Oneness. But this true equality with God distinguishes between thoughts and thinkers. The recognition of God's variety of life, form, color, etc., are each equally necessary to the fulfillment of the Divine plan. This is the only law of equality. Life, thus eternalized, is equality.

Liberty, Fraternity and Equality must ever be the war-cry of the true warrior. But if the offerings, or truths, seen from the watch-tower through the first side of the Fiery Triangle are not acceptable, nor the sacrifices of our past ideas and illusions properly observed or parted with, then, instead of liberty, comes renewed bondage to error and disease; instead of fraternity, failures, strife and murder;

instead of equality with Divinity, there is a descent to the lower sphere and union with demons and fiends.

On the other hand, the Ascetic who mutilates, denies, the truths realized in the major premise from the sentry's watch-tower, and destroys the offerings, the knowledge thus revealed, and who refuses the experiences of the sacrifices can never hear the responses nor know the mystery of re-birth. In either case, remorse and repentance, in themselves, are perfectly stupid, and only delay realization.

The suffering implied in remorse is not a true and acceptable sacrifice, for the major premise is still wrong, for truth never brings remorse. Remorse implies a misconception of the nature of reality. If I have struck the wrong note in my chord, and experienced inharmony, I only make the more haste to strike the right note. I waste no time in groaning over the dismal sound.[148]

LESSON V.

THE EARTHY TRIPLICITY.

♉, OR LISTENING.

The signs of the Earthy Triplicity express the crisis, or fixed point, wherein the shadows seem to come to a crust and harden. They are illusions, reaching their ultimate. And this Earthy Triplicity follows the fiery, just as ashes follow fire, or, as geology tells us, our Earth has resulted from a ball of fire, and all the solids now visible from molten liquids. To the warrior, this Earthy Triplicity (triangle) is the battlefield, a field of three equal sides. Its first side he takes possession of and holds as soon as he comprehends the sounds proceeding from it. He must listen for its strains of martial music, its distant rumbling of artillery and the tramp, tramp of marching troops, its shouts of victory and courage, its groans of anguish, defeat and retreat.

Having learned to watch, he must now learn to listen. The ear must be trained as well as the eye. In order to have both sides of the contradictories we must know the results of things seen, hence must hear the effects through vibration, or motion. Thus listening is essential.

But Taurus ♉ is the sign of the neck and throat as well as the ear, and this is so because of the subtle connection between the ear, neck and throat. In a former analysis I saw the relation of ear to voice (of which the throat is but the instrument), and now, as I listen to the sounds from the battlefield, I discern the relation of ear to neck.

At the first sound of martial music the steed arches his neck, and none the less, as its strains inspire the warrior, does his neck respond to the sounds, drawing up the head and stiffening the entire vertebral column. He pants for prowess, renown, praise, promotion and unending fame and honors. But the true warrior, who from the sentry's watch-tower discerned the shadows to be delusions, now listens for the bugle-call, the clear note which, cleaving the awful din and confusion of the battlefield, gives out the key-note according to which the discordant sounds are evolved into a majestic symphony. As long as the warrior fights for fame of self and to hear all men speak well of him, instead of striking the keynote he only strikes its exact contradictory.

Therefore, if I am to be a true warrior I must renounce praise and learn true humility. Not only must I renounce praise, but must even rejoice when all men speak evil of me. If I am cast down when I am reviled and persecuted, then I have not yet learned humility. To be cut to the quick by censure is as far from humility as to be stiff-necked with praise; for so long as blame crushes me, just so long will praise elate me. Therefore, in order to renounce praise I must also renounce blame.[149]

The point of equilibrium between, or indifference to, either praise or blame is the only point I can strike which will give out the true vibration which enables me to detect the key-note.

This is a hard lesson, and one I can never learn until mine eyes have seen the unreality of the shadows, until I have sacrificed to the Divinity within and obtained its responses; or, in other words, if I have not fully and comprehensively encompassed the first syllogism, or triplicity, I cannot intelligently and courageously step upon the next rung of the ladder in my watch-tower. But if I have realized the war-cry of Liberty, Fraternity and Equality, then, in proportion as I realize humility, renouncing alike praise and blame, in just that proportion I shall now be able to see that my war-cry is also my key-note. I now have my key, which is two-sided, one from the first syllogism and the other from the second, Watching and Listening. This is a marvelous key, which unlocks both ways. Turned one way it reveals color symphonies; the other gives out sound harmonies, and as I become skillful in turning this key the visible will be the notes of a musical composition, which my soul at once reads into sound while the audible vibrations round out into forms and colors. But the visible and the audible united form the Orange Ray of my Seven-Point-Star, and the spiritual quality corresponding to orange is the understanding, and when I am armed with this ray-ment of true understanding, then the bow of prismatic colors and the octave of chromatic sounds will interpret to my soul that larger octave of the heavens called the Zodiac, or Wheel of Life. Upon the steps and half-steps of this Zodiacal octave the Sun, Moon and planets go on, giving out now strong major chords, now plaintive minor vibrations, both of which the rightly attuned soul translates into higher symphonies of the purposes and laws of the Infinite Mind, grand oratorios of "Creation" and "Messiah."

When this spirit of understanding is mine, then these vibrations, struck by the swiftly revolving orbs on the Zodiacal octave, will as surely reach my external ear as they now do my external eye, and my soul will as surely recognize a primary chord from the larger octave as now from the smaller, for the intervals of one correspond exactly to the intervals of the other. All these intervals are expressed by numbers, but as long as numbers represent only dollars and cents, or the shadows exchangeable for money, the results or returns only looked for on the material plane, just so long will the "music of the spheres" remain an unmeaning myth to my soul.

We must ever remember that the effects must correspond to the plane of the cause. Esoteric wisdom cannot be utilized in exoteric gains (the law of contradictory opposites would soon take the place of affinity opposites) and rise in the scale of progress. Harmony is the law of progression. The contest of the ages is upon us.

LESSON VI.

THE EARTHY TRIPLICITY.

♉ ♍ ♑

♍, OR RECONNOITERING.
(PATIENCE — WAIT.)

The green ray is formed by the union of yellow and blue, so the spiritual quality corresponding to green is the blending of the yellow flame, from off the altar of trial and sacrifice, together with the blue of knowledge. The spiritual green resulting from this blending is that peculiar, burning, zealous knowledge which makes the warrior powerful and strong, or, in other words, "mighty in battle."

But the warrior can never be mighty in battle in the midst of wholly unknown country. He must know the mountain passes, the location of bogs and quicksands, rivers and springs. He must understand all the physical and natural advantages and disadvantages of the enemy's position and strongholds, or fortifications. And all this can be accomplished only by the union of skill (knowledge, blue) with daring (sacrifice, yellow). The union of these two results in green of power, a kind of knowing by which the whole vast field of warfare stands out, illuminated, to the mind's eye of the warrior. Now the work of mixing together skill and daring, by means of which the country becomes known, is the work of reconnoitering.

Reconnoitering is therefore the subject of this lesson and the second side of my triangle. In planning for the work in hand I must first draw upon the knowledge already obtained of this perilous region of shadows and illusions.

Virgo is the symbol for the process of assimilation, which takes place in the intestines, or bowels, and if this process be incomplete or inharmonious, loss of strength is the immediate result. I become weak-kneed, unable to walk or even stand. Just so our Mother Earth (the Green Planet) has stored away for the use of her children, down in the caverns and spacious recesses of her bowels, a vast and complete laboratory, with all materials and chemical appliances at hand where daring reconnoiterers become the daring alchemists. Knowledge has been gained, and power obtained through assimilation to put that knowledge into practical use.

But where are those who do not assimilate the food provided by Mother Nature, who are indifferent to conditions, and fail to see and hear, who lack that burning zeal to reconnoiter so that they may make themselves acquainted with the various aspects of the country, hence fall into the refuse bogs and morasses and lose what strength they do have, become unable to walk, or even stand, and are finally cast out into the outer darkness of nothingness? Our Mother Earth is a just planet, and no goodie-goodie, stuffing obedient and disobedient alike with confectionery. Each attracts to himself the just compensation for the energy put forth, whether that be much or little, good or evil.

If I am deceived by the will-o'-the-wisps, or follow wandering doctrines, not only must I ask to be forgiven for my trespasses, but I am also sure to suffer some punishment or reprimand for my mistakes. Yet, if I am wise, I accept them thankfully and cheerfully, without repining, for thus are accomplished two things: First, the suffering is the healing remedy, which repairs the mischief; second, just as the mother takes more closely to her heart than ever before the truly penitent child, just so Mother Earth reveals her most precious secrets to her right-minded offspring, those who are patient under suffering and affliction and learn the lessons of remorse, suffering and humility, knowing that Nature is only asking, or demanding, a just retribution for violation of her laws. Ignorance excuses not. Nothing but knowledge can enable one to escape the bogs and morasses of ignorance.

And thus right here, I see, comes the application of my lesson on the discipline of the ear. Reconnoitering puts to the test listening, or true humility. If the first and the second sides of this Earthy triangle are rightly constructed, then the second note of the chord will harmonize with the first, and I know that so far my work is well done.

But if I find discord, then it is an absolute certainty that the third side of my triangle will not fit, and if I undertake to advance upon the enemy's territory, swift and sure defeat is before me. Therefore in all humility I set diligently to work to construct a map of the country I am about to invade, and procure a compass, so that I may not lose my way amidst the false doctrines which encompass me on every hand, at every turn, and the dense forests of "isms," which bewilder and perplex.

This compass is but a simple Cross, which always points to the Pole-Star of Truth, arid indicates the four cardinal points of the Universe, and the fourfold division of both Macrocosm and Microcosm.

Aries, the Fiery, rules the Eastern terminus of this Rosy-Cross; Libra, the Airy, the Western; Capricorn, the Earthy (the most fixed and material), the Southern, while Cancer, the Watery, pure desire, forever aspires to the North of Truth and Freedom.

Thus the four points of the compass also express the four elements. Each element also expresses the fourfold constitution of man: Earth, Body; Fire, Finite Mind, or Fiery Body; Water, Soul; Air, Spirit.

There is nothing so penetrating as air, and no element so essential to life. In every form of life air is the potent, animating principle, and without the air (spirit) the other four elements would be useless.

The spirit is one and indivisible, but the other three divisions of man are each dual, and thus results the sevenfold division of the Microcosm, or, going back to the four elements, I can regard each as triune, and from this division map out the Zodiac, this mazy wheel of life, and thus completing the reconnoiter of my great field of battle I boldly advance, clinging to my simple Solar Cross.

LESSON VII.

THE EARTHY TRIPLICITY.

♉ ♍ ♑

♑, OR ADVANCING.

When the Sun enters the sign of ♑, where lived the framers of the Zodiac, then the Goats advanced up the mountain sides, for the time of grazing was at hand. The fruits of labor were beginning to spring up and be realized by the laborer. So now advances the warrior into the region of winter, toward the point where shadows are congealed or hardened into the substances called matter and solids; where the indigo ray passes almost to black — the exact antipodes of soul and summer, the white light. Here the black of negation mixes with blue to form the indigo of righteousness.

But with his faithful compass (Cross) he advances, undismayed. His knees do not knock together through the weakness of fear; fear belongs to immature natures. The patient waiting acquired as a reconnoiterer has admitted him into the laboratory of Mother Earth, and he has there armed himself with the force which solves solids and transmutes matter into its correlatives of spirit — black to white, death to life.

The Rod and the Knee express the two extremes of Power and Submission. The monarch who sways the rod enforces the homage of the bended knee from his subjects. Never was there such a despot as fear, and the victim swayed by fear is the most craven and knock-kneed object in existence. The one who has not learned to wait is still the slave of fear, and is held bound in the bowels of Earth, and has yet to break the bars of iron and steel which hold him a prisoner of pomp, splendor, honor and dignity, and this also implies its exact opposite. Yet, the one whom the world delights to honor is not the one who advances, a conqueror, into the realm of realities. Ah, no! He is the one most overcome by fear and that grim, monster-shadow called Death. But the true warrior, "compass" in hand, even though despised and rejected by men advances undismayed, knowing before-hand the exact nature of that which he is to explore. He knows the grim monster-shadow, death, to be but Nature's initiation into the great mysteries of existence, whose realms he, like Virgil and Dante and others before him, have invaded while yet embodied.

He will find it possible to go, and, returning, give a clever and entertaining account of adventures, hairbreadth escapes, etc., to a gaping crowd. He may bring back a lot of curios, to dispose of for money to the highest bidder, for curiosity mongers to "Oh!" and "Ah!" over.

Or he may transform his knowledge into a comfortable "Sale of Indulgences," proclaim: "There is no such thing as Death; he is only a scarecrow; all is life; there is no such thing as Evil, all is good. Therefore gormandize, cheat and steal to your heart's content. You are one with God, and your soul can never be lost!" But he strikes a note which grates on the purely trained ear, and he communicates a conclusion which does not accord with, nor follow, the premises. With the major premise of Taurus (humility) and the minor premise of Virgo (patience), sooner or later will he trip in the meshes of his false syllogism and be brought in abject terror before the awful

Voice of the Mighty One, whose Ineffable Name he, himself, has attempted to assume, instead of, in true humility, saying " Hallowed be Thy Name," and, as a penitent reconnoiterer, he must add, " Forgive us our trespasses," and upon his knees confess, "For Thine is the Kingdom."

But not thus with the warrior who has the first two premises correctly formed. His conclusion is incontrovertible. At the very outset of his advance he learns his immortality, his heritage; also discerns the conditions upon which they are won. He realizes the dignity, grandeur and meaning of life, and knows that he is saved, crowned and Deified in spite of himself; whether he will or no. Neither for the simple wishing on his part, but with the knowledge obtained in Dame Nature's laboratory he has but to hold up the Mystic Cross, which combines in its significance polar opposites and contradictory opposites, and the most fixed becomes volatile. Baser metals are changed to gold, and gold transmuted to Sunlight, the Water of Soul to the Wine of Spirit, the mask to reality, shadows to substance, error to truth, hate to love, death to life.

He also knows that the direct ray is Truth Absolute, while the oblique ray is Truth Relative, and will be refracted and reflected indefinitely from one plane to another and soon bewilder him in a labyrinth of shadowy reflects unless he sternly adheres to his knowledge and boldly clings to his Cross.

And, while he knows that it is his duty to realize and actualize all that he possibly can of truth absolute, he also knows it is likewise his duty to recognize the different planes of expression, and remember that truths on different planes are relative to each other, but that each is absolute on its own plane, and that, in order to advance from one plane to another, or higher, like water he cannot rise above his level until he find the point of equilibrium of that plane upon which he is, by means of which, like water vaporized, he rises to the plane above him.

But, until he does actually rise to the plane above him, he is ruled by the laws of that plane, and he is its subject until he, by rising to the plane above, becomes ruler of the plane below.

Poison, calumny and malice are absolute monarchs on their own special plane, but to the warrior, armed with the force which solves and transmutes, they become relative, and finally obedient.

Neither do I become ruler by simply repeating, parrot-like, "There is no such thing as malaria; malaria does not rule me, I rule malaria," etc., but I must have within me the force which, having divined the meanings of things, has made them a part of me, having neutralized (nothing-ized) it by counterbalancing it with its polar opposite.

Thus, from ♑ of the Earthy Triplicity, do I arrive at true Progress, Advancing. The Fiery trip showed the perfect syllogism — the righteous judgment of Sagittarius, deducted from the major premise of Aries and the minor premise of Leo.

The Earthy syllogism, analogous to the Fiery, is symbolized in terms of a chemical compound, in which the sharp and stinging acids of censure and uncharitableness, leading to humility (Taurus), fuse and blend with the alkalies of patience (Virgo) under afflictions, and from this fusing and blending arising to a higher plane, or Capricorn.

From this Earthy syllogism I have learned from Taurus: "Hark!" from Virgo: "Wait!" from Capricorn: "Be Strong!"

Listening in true Humility for Thy hallowed name, I have found that even sorrow and failure, if accepted in patience, although they may seem like the reconnoiterer's path, too often go back instead of forward, are, after all, accomplished progress, and are but seeming bonds, from which my soul, "like a hind let loose" all the more swiftly advances up the mountain steeps when the time for grazing arrives. Then he has reached that point where he can utilize the power and knowledge gained while passing through the first syllogism, Fire, and the second, Earth.

LESSON VIII.

THE AIRY TRIPLICITY.

♊ ♎ ♒

♊, OR CARRYING ARMS.

The signs of the Airy Triplicity have especial reference to motion. ♊, more especially, or directly, is concerned with projecting, hurling, etc.; ♎ with balancing, maintaining equilibrium between opposites; ♒ with floating and undulating, as represented by the action of air upon the surface of the water, producing waves.

♊ implies, first, a grasping of the hands, or combining forces (Gemini), the effects of knowledge gained so far on his journey; second, an impulsive force from the will, directed to the muscles of the shoulders and arms, by means of which the object is hurled through the air. Therefore I can be no warrior and hurl my lance until I understand the meaning of these twins and how to train and use them effectually.

First, I discern that these twins are not two of the same kind, but they are opposites, or counterparts, and fit together like two hemispheres of one sphere. The one is right, the other left; the one positive, the other negative.

Ancient mythology allegorized one, the right half, the positive, as Castor, a star of the first magnitude, the Immortal, while the other, the left, the negative, was Pollux, the lesser star in brilliancy, the Mortal; and thus they expressed the fact that it is the positive, active force of the soul which, reaching out, attains immortality; i. e., there must be action before there could be reaction. But, again, as the action itself must have its reaction in order to complete its orbit, as the positive pole of the battery is nothing without its negative pole, just so the immortal Castor is represented in the myth as one-half of the time foregoing his privilege among the Celestials in order to pass the other half of the time with his brother, who was mortal, yet whom he so dearly loved; or, in other words, they were polar opposites, which mutually implied each other, and were utterly meaningless and unthinkable apart.

(And one quite noticeable fact of twins is that, even while of the same sex physically, in temperament and disposition one is more positive, the other more negative. Usually this difference is very marked.)

In regard to the hands, I observe that, while the right is positive to the left, yet the different parts of each hand are relatively positive and negative to each other, Thus the knuckles are positive in relation to the palm, the nails positive in relation to the balls of the fingers, etc. The elbows are aggressive, while the muscles of the inner arm are indrawing and caressive.

The hands are the great avenues of the sense of touch. The hands are the means by which we grasp at treasures, reach out for that which we wish to attain, manipulate, formulate materials about us in order to provide for the necessities, comforts and luxuries of physical life.

And from these two, following the law of correspondences, I discern the esoteric meaning of the hands, and from thence the application of bearing arms. The right hand has been educated almost to the exclusion of the left (or female) in our present generation. Otherwise it would be self-evident to us that sensation is not completely obtained only through the right, and when we examine anything critically we instinctively use both hands. Our right hand gives us more the external, intellectual, positive qualities of an object, the left the interior, intuitional, negative qualities; and thus the first great use of the hands is to teach polar opposites, the Twins. All the infinite variety of weapons or arms the warrior can ever have to deal with can be classed under these two words — Polar Opposites. Every force throughout the boundless universe has its pole, or Divine center, which embraces the positive and negative attributes in one, and in order to correspond to that pole all life is evolved in pairs — twins, male and female. Whenever they appear to be separated it is only in seeming, and because the external eye is blinded to the shadow of illusions.

Again, just as we have neglected the education of the left hand, just so have we lost, through this neglect, that inner consciousness of the esoteric meaning of the thousands of exoteric, or physical, uses with which we daily employ our hands. Our treasures are accumulated only for this world, regardless of the swift-coming subjective state, upon whose borders we may this very instant be drifting.

This, then, is the lesson for the warrior. The arms of warfare are polar opposites. Bearing arms is learning their esoteric uses.

Right here, for the warrior, must come his great renunciation. He must come to care for the external only for the sake of the interior. He must "renounce luxury and be chaste." But chastity is by no means celibacy nor asceticism. For the true soul love is in very truth the purest chastity.

The word chaste is here, however, used in its true and larger sense. Polar opposites is only another word for sex; hence the word chaste applies to every word and ought.

Let the warrior, then, cleanse his hands and remember that the blessings of the Lord are promised to one who "hath clean hands and a pure heart."

The force which binds polar opposites together, the point of equilibrium where the two are one, is love, and from love is evolved life, while truth may be defined as knowledge, or understanding, of the relation of polar opposites. The warrior must first comprehend truth, and truth must be in him and he in the truth before he can possibly know anything whatever of life and of love. But he must renounce the things of sense and seeming in order to say: u Oh, Truth! Thy Kingdom Come."

But it directly follows the fact of the uneducated left hand, and the consequent non-comprehension of polar opposites, that mankind to-day can have no conception whatever of the Law of Unity, or the love by which the two polar opposites are one. And thus the world has utterly lost the esoteric meaning of the love which exists exoterically between man and woman. Marriage is only a name and a form, a legal, conventional and mechanical union, and the empty symbol no longer teaches the spiritual reality.[150] With the Divine element of love lost to our sight, atheism and materialism at once follow. The days of true chivalry are the days of true religious growth.

Man cannot know God without knowing love, for God is love, and if the exoteric symbol of love does not lead to an insight to spiritual truth, to an actual knowledge of truth (which is also God), then that exoteric symbol is the grossest unchastity, and leads to perdition and damnation.

But the warrior, having put aside, or renounced, all the showy and glittering weapons of sense and seeming, arming himself only with truth, as symbolized in his lance, with its two ends, and, balancing this trusty lance in his hands, he discerns the sublime truth of the Twins (II), and knows that somewhere in the vast universe there exists a missing half, from whom his soul, in reality, never has been and never can be separated.

LESSON IX.

THE AIRY TRIPLICITY.

♊ ♎ ♒

♎, OR OBEYING ORDERS.

The spirit of mortal, alas, is proud. Not realizing itself as nothing but a shadowy reflect, it arrogates to itself, while yet a minor, its birthright of Divinity and heritage of immortality, as if it had already attained its majority and come into possession of its estate.

Obedience is a difficult attainment, perhaps the most difficult of all, and yet all the boasted free will of a mortal ends in his obedience, in spite of himself, for one grand command comprises all the lesser orders. The others are but copies, or reprints, of the original.

This One Supreme is that Divine love principle which binds polar opposites into one. And true is the command: " What God hath joined together let no man put asunder," for mortal cannot put it asunder. He cannot accomplish the impossible and unthinkable, and there is but one punishment for attempted disobedience. He does not alter the law, but, as far as he himself is concerned, he realizes the results in accordance with his disregard of the law, whether intentional or not.

To fulfill this great law of love is peace, equilibrium, harmony and life; to ignore or defy it is strife, confusion, discord and death.

And thus the mortal obeys the law in spite of himself, for death is not a change preparatory to another state or condition of life, in which the mortal, or reflect, is given another chance to obey the order which comprises all orders.

THE EQUILIBRIUM OR EQUALITY OF RATIOS.

Love.

♎

Justice.

In walking, which is propelling the body through the air, the process of locomotion is threefold, or triune; i. e., there are three great centers of locomotion. First, the arms and shoulders; second, the legs, especially the muscles of the calves, and the third is that portion of the body which is the point of equilibrium between the two, and this portion perfectly describes an old-fashioned balance, or pair of scales, ♎. It includes the reins, or kidneys, and extends to the loins, or hips. Now, in walking, as the weight of the body is thrown on one leg the opposite hip, like one end of the beam of the scales, comes up and the other hip goes down, then vice versa, and so on. This is so in true, natural walking; but alas! the fine, true, harmonious, stately gait is very rare in this degenerate age. Yet if this perfect equipoise of the body were maintained at every step, walking could be continued indefinitely without fatigue.

But to one who understands the esoteric meaning of symbols there can be no more significant and saddening sight than to watch for a moment the hurrying, swaying, shuffling throng of a crowded street.

Truly is the world blind to the knowledge of soul poise, and disobedient to the law which binds polar opposites into a unity.

On the reflected and phenomenal plane this law has special reference to the forms of union called marriage and partnership. The same law which governs marriage governs partnership, no matter whether the parties are composed of nations or only two individuals, and looking out into the world to-day, with its teeming millions, a very serious state of affairs is presented to the eyes of the warrior.

Inharmony, discord, strife everywhere. No marriage, all lust; no partnership, all monopoly. And nowhere is this more apparent than among those who profess to have found Truth — to know the real from the unreal.

However, as the warrior rises to a higher plane, and regards the present condition of humanity in a larger sense, he only sees them with pitying and tender eyes, as infants learning to walk, tottering, and in constant danger of losing their balance; swayed first by one strong passion and then another, and then he knows just how far it is possible for one soul to help another — only in so far as a child can be helped to walk. But the child must walk for itself; no one can walk for it. I can, by my understanding of truth, influence another person to do a virtuous deed. This deed would be the result of an action on my part; so, unless there is also a reaction on the part of the person performing the deed, there has been no equilibrium established whereby any inner purity has been evolved on his part, and he has not, consciously, taken a single step for himself toward truth. I have only lifted him up and carried him, and perhaps delayed him in the process of walking. He will look for some one else walking for himself. The soul cannot grow vicariously, anymore than the child can so walk.

Now this belief in the possibility of a vicarious union of polar opposites, or At-one-ment, is the great delusion of the age. Truly there is but one way under the Sun whereby men can be saved. It is by obedience to the law of equilibrium. Not a stupid, passive obedience, for, like everything else under the Sun, obedience is dual — active and passive, positive and negative. Therefore, while I accept the fact that every soul must walk for itself, yet at the same time I remember that it must have its seeming props and helps, while learning to walk, until it attains its majority. So I must help all about me. Thus, for the time being, I seem to hinder, but only in order to help. This is that awful law of contradictories, so bewildering to the child soul, wherein we seemingly disobey in order to obey. Herein consists the duality of obedience. In order to realize absolute good I must, for the time being, accept relative, or seeming, evil; but it is only in accordance with the higher law, which evolves the perfect harmony out of seeming discord, whereby I gain my spiritual insight and read aright the esoteric meaning from the exoteric symbol. If I accept seeming evil for any other purpose, I am at once bound in chains of sense and seeming and sink deeper and deeper in the shadows, until that which should be a symbol for the very highest, following the law of contradictories, becomes the very lowest and foulest, as is now so generally the case with symbolic marriages.

In the particular phase of soul unfoldment through which humanity is at present passing, the last and highest symbol for mortal to comprehend is marriage — the union of man and woman. The very fact that there is a symbol proves there is a reality. The fact of a shadow proves there must be a substance. Just so the exoteric form we know as marriage proves, of necessity, a true soul marriage, and further, for the warrior this is a most significant fact and means another lesson, which cannot be omitted. The reason this At-one-ment is seldom or never realized is, as we have just seen, humanity has not yet developed to the point of soul equilibrium. It cannot yet walk; therefore this soul union can only take place in the next phase or condition of development. Man can no more realize soul marriage than our domestic animals could live our present family life.

But right here, at this point, the warrior who has mastered the former lessons, stands forth in the strength of his God-given heritage, scorning the shadow symbols, determined to know only the real; he foregoes all the sensuous and seeming and becomes the true celibate. He sees that one of the factors in the attainment of his celestial heritage is the union with his polar opposite. The immortality of his soul is an utter unthinkability without this At-one-ment. He can never come into possession of his Kingdom until he places a Queen upon the Throne by his side. He cannot be knighted until he has found and won his lady. Thus is he justified in putting aside earthly ties, only in order to realize the celestial union which follows obedience to the love which binds together polar opposites.

LESSON X.

THE AIRY TRIPLICITY.

♊ ♎ ♒

♒, OR PROVIDING RATIONS.

The three duties of Bearing Arms, Obeying Orders and Providing Rations, comprised under the Airy Triplicity, relate more to the special training and individual discipline of the warrior, yet none the less necessary and important to his success, for the properly drilled and thoroughly disciplined warrior, having completed the three sides of the Airy Triplicity, stands forth as the wonder-working magician, able to transform light into the bread of Heaven, or the power to put into use the knowledge gained.

First, if he knows how to bear arms, i. e., to properly formulate with his esoteric hands; second, if he has thoroughly vitalized his purposes from a strict obedience to the laws of polar opposites and equilibrium; third, then he has only to strike the third note of the chord to realize his undertakings completed and actualized, and himself nourished and sustained as are the angels of light themselves.

Properly formulated and vitalized, his thoughts cannot return unto him void. Herein is the awful, the divinely and unspeakably awful force of this law of equilibrium or balance. They cannot return void, and if they have been revengeful, malicious or covetous, and have worked out results of sorrow and suffering to others, then, as he has measured so will it be measured out to him. Sooner or later will they complete their orbit and find him out. Polar opposites, vitalized, are the same things as centrifugal and centripetal forces set in motion. They will describe a circle. Mortal cannot annul Divine law.

The warrior has now reached a point where he must become a breadmaker. First, the loaves must be kneaded and formulated with the hands ($\mathbb{I}$); second, the loaves must be vitalized, fomented by an understanding of ($\underline{\Omega}$) the equipoise of the two opposite forms of force, in order that, third, he may realize himself nourished and sustained and finally thus self- sustaining ($\approx$) .

His bread must be either life-giving or life-destroying, for, once formulated and fomented (vitalized), his loaves cannot return to him void.

It is perfectly possible for him to formulate expressions or images for what is absolutely impossible and unthinkable. It is also possible for him to seemingly vitalize his phantoms, but the awful results of this kind of breadmaking are sure to follow. His phantoms become vampires, which feed upon him, and even upon all who ignorantly come within his mental atmosphere. Yet this possibility must not deter the warrior, for he must be a breadmaker. He must put into practical use that which he has made himself acquainted with; he must let his cup overflow, so as to benefit those who walk with him. Inaction is as fatal as to create vampires for unthinkables and impossibilities. Therefore, let the work rely upon the purity of his motive, which is soul unfoldment and the attainment of his celestial heritage knowing that, sooner or later, the law will be revealed to him from within, how those loaves which turn out failures and abortions can be neutralized and nothingized.

If he is free from covetousness, vainglory and sensuousness, then let him work only to know truth and realize justice, and he will find himself self-sustaining and able to command in emergencies, and finally find within himself an image of that creative force which, in its turn, images the Divine creative will, or center of the universe.

This law of the creative, or bread-making, syllogism is universal in its application, from the most seeming and external life up to the highest symbolic form of our present phase of Earth life, or child creating, in which the human approaches the nearest to the Divine parent.

To a certain extent, the warrior must have a varied and large experience throughout all the worlds of form-making. He must work unceasingly, as does the Great Creator. Herein is the import of the command to be "fruitful, increase and multiply;" not that man and woman are to devote their whole time, thought and energies to populating the globe, as the selfish sensualist proclaims from the house-top in order to procure a license for his own secret sins, but through that equilibrium gained by the harmonious blending and fusing of polar opposites, or twin souls.

His thoughts, truths, or bread, will be his children, who will guide and sustain him as well as those who partake of such royal dainties, born from the union of formulation and vitalization. Thus the bread-winner becomes the bread-distributor, and the loaves of understanding will not be void.

The consciousness of his dual self evolved through his journey on the first side of the Airy Triangle [♊], and where he learns to formulate, and on the second side ([♎]), where the creative principles are balanced — then, and not until then, does he become capable of breadmaking, or creating self-sustenance; and when he is able and strong enough to walk alone he must support others, for we cannot receive unless we also give. Thenceforward the warrior can enjoy the promise of his Creator: "For whosoever hath, to him shall be given, and he shall have more abundance; but whosoever hath not, from him shall be taken away even that he hath," and cast forth upon the universal currents the life-sustaining rations of his own winning, not in floods or great downpours, but as the gentle, soothing, rippling waves of ([♒]).

In bearing arms the warrior is subject to the higher commands of his being, and is, in action, manipulated by the arms — not the arm, but the arms, implying the utter uselessness of one alone. The brave, positive Castor must be balanced by his mate, Pollux; thus the training and culture necessary for bearing arms correctly, as a skilled warrior, every movement known, and at what moment to so execute the laws of his will that they will not conflict with Nature's laws and bring failure and sorrow for his ignorant disobedience.

Herein self is forgotten, self is lost in the recognition of the two as one, equalized, blended as one.

This awful mystery of self, this life-destroying monster, when alone, stalking about as the imperious I. Selfishness of the past must be lost, for now he becomes the man; that selfishness that ruled and regulated the life of the lower forms through which the soul was gaining experience before the plane of reason and intuition had been reached, and then only can perfect obedience and equilibrium be attained.

Bearing arms is wearisome, obeying orders difficult, and demands an indefatigable exercise in Watching, Listening and patient advancement that the balance is not tilted by misjudgements.

Then the warrior can traverse his kingdom and scan the circumference of his ground in so far as he has reached in his watch-tower. More climbing is to be done, hence sustenance is required; therefore he must utilize his balanced forces and provide his own self-sustaining rations. Another's winnings or knowledge would not sustain and give him the freedom in exploring his universe in search of the object of his journey — Truth.

What constitute the Rations?
The attributes evolved on each side of the four equilateral triangles of Fire, Air, Earth and Water.

Providing Rations is externalizing the twelve manners of fruits, each division of his own kingdom providing the necessary material.

The truths that spring from every side of the triangles in the fourfold elements are food and sustenance to his soul.

His journey is not yet complete. He is now in the realm of Imagery. Knowledge and experience are necessary in this creative realm.

He must bear arms with caution. The Lance of Light and Truth must be borne aloft constantly, that impossible imageries may not be formulated and spring into active expression to impede his progress.

His desires and loyal aspirations make him charitable to all life. Yet the true warrior must not hesitate at sacrifices. He must become master of his own kingdom, hence must make the lives born from his own thoughts subject and useful to his Divine will.

The higher he ascends into the tower the brighter becomes his Ray of Light, the expanse of country broader, and new things appear to his vision, new conditions present themselves. A new stimulus to action is received. Responsibility is increased and more knowledge is required, and ever on and on.

Life is motion, as the Airy Triplicity symbolizes, and motion is eternal.

LESSON XI.

THE WATERY TRIPLICITY.

♋ ♏ ♓

♋, OR ASPIRING.

The signs of the Watery Triplicity are pre-eminently fruitful signs, and, just as all physical germination, growth, prosperity, maternity and fruition depend for their existence on water, so must the germ seeds of aspiration be moistened by the waters of spiritual life before they will germinate and bear us outward fruit; and we may go further, and say that the very first primordial germ of organic life itself, in the first faint blush of the dawn of God's creation, had its origin in the element known as water. So, on the higher planes of living there must be the Water of Life, the springs and fountains of which sustain soul fruition.

Desire is the first side of the fruitful triangle, that which the soul ardently longs for, that which the soul will fight for until all obstacles are vanquished, but when there is no desire the soul seed will attract no moisture to enable it to send forth its tiny shoots up toward the Sunlight of Truth.

Yet, to the truly aspiring soul this Water of Life is not anything external to the soul itself. On the contrary, it is the very element which, self-generating, flows like an ocean of Infinite love from the celestial, Deific center of its birthplace onward and downward through myriads of solar centers and starry systems until it reaches its perihelion point upon some earth, the external battle ground of matter, whereon it enters the good fight against the blind force of lower nature, to return at the ebb of its own celestial tide, triumphant, through countless spiritual states and spheres of glorious, pulsating life.

Aspiring is breathing, and true breathing creates an atmosphere about the soul germ which will in itself collect together moisture and generate the seed.

The seed that is planted at the proper cyclic period can, through desire and aspiration, be watered from time to time until the harvest is most bountiful.

Born in water, nourished with water, dissolved again in water, to be born upon higher planes of life. Existence is eternal, but spheres and planes are eternally changing. Promotion is the law of God, and the warrior can, by his own efforts, shorten his warfare upon the battle ground of materiality by becoming familiar with his own country, and, through the knowledge of its layout, the points of vantage and disadvantage, he can soon rise to the apex of the Watery Triangle. Cancer represents on the Earth the oceans and their correspondences, the broad expanse of the spiritual Water of Life on the spiritual plane. Here the soul is nearing the Divine center of its being. True inspiration here takes place, that Divine respiration, where each inhalation and exhalation is in harmony with the ebb and flow of the tides of spiritual life. Hence inspiration naturally belongs to the signs of the Watery Triplicity.

The natural moisture that will bring forth to external life the latent possibilities, or seeds of the soul, is desire, aspirations and creations from material (knowledge) accumulated while traversing the battle ground up to the present plane of warfare.

Through the Water of Life knowledge has been born on the journey, so that his bread is the knowledge of good and evil, of polar opposites, and when his eyes take the observations of the flights of the birds the law of contradictories will direct his judgments and his movements.

He has learned the law governing the blind forces of Nature, and now, instead of obeying their orders, he, himself, has become the triumphant master of these forces, and the elements, as well, as the elementals, of each realm are now his servants and slaves, moving and obeying is kingly commands.

Another step is taken in the watchtower, and so cautiously has he moved over his ground, and so thoroughly mastered every condition as he proceeded, that now he is monarch of all he surveys from the point of observation that he has reached, and rightly earned, in his fearless march through the field of battle.

He now knows the extent of his immediate battle ground, the force of the enemy, the obstacles to surmount, the fortifications to throw up; but, being armed with the Lance of Truth and Knowledge and his path illuminated by his Ray-of- Light, he prepares to descend from his tower and take full possession of his country, or his own individual universe, and, with his queen. The natural moisture that will bring forth to external life the latent possibilities, or seeds of the soul, is desire, aspirations and creations from material (knowledge) accumulated while traversing the battle ground up to the present plane of warfare.

Through the Water of Life knowledge has been born on the journey, so that his bread is the knowledge of good and evil, of polar opposites, and when his eyes take the observations of the flights of the birds the law of contradictories will direct his judgments and his movements.

He has learned the law governing the blind forces of Nature, and now, instead of obeying their orders, he, himself, has become the triumphant master of these forces, and the elements, as well, as the elementals, of each realm are now his servants and slaves, moving and obeying his kingly commands.

Another step is taken in the watch-tower, and so cautiously has he moved over his ground, and so thoroughly mastered every condition as he proceeded, that now he is monarch of all he surveys from the point of observation that he has reached, and rightly earned, in his fearless march through the field of battle.

He now knows the extent of his immediate battle ground, the force of the enemy, the obstacles to surmount, the fortifications to throw up; but, being armed with the Lance of Truth and Knowledge and his path illuminated by his Ray-of- Light, he prepares to descend from his tower and take full possession of his country, or his own individual universe, and, with his queen, reign supreme.

"Give us this day our daily food" is herein signified, and it must be drawn by the Divine Center of our being from the infinite ocean of spiritual life.

Man can draw, through respiration, all the moisture he wishes to nourish the seeds of immortal life.

The breathing known by all true warriors, that breathing of soul to soul, of God to Man, of Man to Woman, of Infinite to Finite, of Great to Small, is the harmonious relationship of polar opposites, and soul affinities will bring the requisite harmony and union of the finite to the infinite.

The perfect response of the body to mind, when the interior and exterior breathing is going on alternately, will set the soul free to soar aloft amidst its own special sphere of life, to grow and gain knowledge of its own in the realm of realities, that he may learn their laws, and thus become the master of their reflections on the battlefield of matter.[151]

The wielding of the scepter of aspiration calls forth inspiration, and sets in motion the creative power of thought. Here, again, the warrior is cautioned, in his work of creation, that he create not impossibilities and unthinkabilities, lest they become unconquerable foes on other planes, or rounds, of the esoteric ladder.

Is the warrior to create new forms of life, that will prove willing slaves or rebellious tyrants in his kingdom?

This is a portion of his breadmaking.

This is a generous realm, where the vibrations are set up by the soul's ardent desires and aspirations, and the creations are limited only by the will.

If he has not learned how to watch and wait, listen, and obey the God within, stumbling blocks will surely arise at an unguarded moment, and be as fungi in his kingdom when taking form on the second side of the triangle of this triplicity.

In no realm is the reconnoiterer to be more guarded in his movements, for creation follows every action. The Lance is here needed to put to instant flight the false imaginings of the soul before being vitalized and taking on form.

LESSON XII.

THE WATERY TRIPLICITY.

♋ ♏ ♓

♏ OR ATTACKING.

The early morning of the great day has at length arrived. The hour so long awaited and so carefully prepared for has come, and the warrior now descends from the heights of his watch-tower, armed with the Ray-of-Light of Lance and Knowledge to meet the enemies of the battle ground. The war-cry is sounded, and echoed from center to circumference.

He has descended into matter, into the shadows of nothingness, but from this plane they are real as long as the shadow lasts.

He steps forward, well armed, and the first phantom to conquer and put to flight is Self. Fear is the shadow of the real man. He must be fearless, for " he who hesitates is lost." Caution guides his steps, and his lamp, or Divine Ray, illumines his path. Step by step he progresses; foes, real and unreal, are met with unyielding will, and a determination to return home the Master, the King, the Lord and Ruler of his own Kingdom. All must be brought to obedience and service of his Divine will.

Not forgetting the possibility of slipping too far on either side of the point of balance and becoming a tyrant on the one hand or a slave on the other, he keeps keenly alive to all conditions and wide-awake to all temptations that might prove pitfalls or unconquerable obstacles, and thus losing the freedom he seeks.

He is now traversing and experiencing another angle of the Watery Triangle — the realm of creative forms. On this side of the triangle is the fierce struggle for life going on. Life is sweet to the lowest forms of existence, and the battle to defend and preserve it is a battle to the death. This the warrior seeks to avoid — the premature cutting off of life, for that would rob him of their service and his rule.

Utilization is the secret of success, not waste nor abandon.

The greatest wisdom must be displayed in this realm of creation, where man imitates or obeys the command of his God: "Increase, multiply and replenish the Earth" — not with false images, that will eventually take form and become the shadows on the plane of matter, but truths, that will be solid stepping stones to higher rounds of being, and be of that nature where he can set them up as mile-stones to guide correctly the travelers who may follow him in adjoining countries.

The life-giving force that is generated on this side of the triangle is threefold in its influence and power of utilization.

Does the warrior want all his creations in material forms? Does he want only the fruits of matter, that so soon perish? Does he want to be buried in nothingness, from which eternal things cannot be born? No!

Allurements of the shadows are great, and he must constantly pray: "Lead us not into temptation." The Balance must be brought into constant use, the Magic Lance ever borne aloft, so that in an unguarded moment he may not lose his way and be overcome by the snares ever lurking on this side of the triangle.

His first formulations, or conceptions, are here to take form and become active, living realities upon or in his kingdom.

Here comes the test of his work in the realms visible. The mystical sign of this Triplicity is revealed to the warrior as he enters its sphere. Unknown and undreamed-of trials and temptations, real and apparent obstacles will spring up at every step as he goes forth to attack, subdue, conquer and master.

To master is the watchword of the true warrior, knowing that in the sacrifice of forms new lives spring into existence, more formidable than those he sacrifices.

It is man's duty to evolve, not destroy, and his creations must have the wings of the eagle, to bear them aloft above the illusions of matter.

Here the mind rises superior to the lower self; the lower must and will become the servant of the higher. Terrible will be the attack; not a moment must he rest; looking back will be fatal. In no part of the warfare must one stand so resolute, so steadfast, so courageous. No other part of the field is so boggy. The creations of sense and seeming are his enemies. No part of the journey is so full of rebellion, warring incessantly, until the whole circumference encircling his dominions is encompassed.

The vantage is not great in the realm ruled by Scorpio. The spark of light at the point of his lance will not pierce the darkness far, but each advancing step drives back to humble submission the lurking forms of the shadows.

At last what transpires? Instead of the creeping, slimy serpent, the aspirations have given it wings. The Scorpion has been transformed. It is now the eagle, able to soar in the water of the Infinite Waters of Life instead of creeping upon the battle ground of matter.

The work is done. The innocent, ignorant warrior returns the conqueror. He is bid to come up higher, and again he ascends to the top of his watch-tower and awaits his heritage.

LESSON XIII.

THE WATERY TRIPLICITY.

♋ ♏ ♓

♓, OR VANQUISHING.

As the mists and the shadows of the battlefield clear away the warrior pauses, and from his height views the mighty field of conflict and weighs and considers the results from the twelve mansions of his dominion. Each has been penetrated and the fruits gathered and garnered and he has partaken thereof. The illusions and delusions of the battlefield have been perceived and their nothingness realized, and the warrior has now to vanquish them by the laws he has learned in watching, listening, patient and cautious advancement and reconnoitering, aspiring while attacking, and in his engagements in battle.

He has plenty of time to reflect while the atmosphere is clearing. His journey has led him to the last rung of the exoteric ladder.

The mists of seeming and sense begin to pass away, all preconceptions have vanished, he has climbed the exoteric ladder, and now he is about to face the realms of realities and to place his foot upon the first rung of the esoteric ladder.

Has he been released from all exoteric burdens, his bundles of loves, of hates, of revenge, of false conceptions and conclusions that were drawn from the realm of effects and dropped by the wayside? These are the mists and shadows of the battlefield, that have clung so tenaciously to the warrior's outward self.

What are the considerations of his reflections?

Knowledge has been his lot and portion, and he is now fitted to proclaim his kingship, his queen by his side, the equilibrium gained, the fight for freedom won.

Having triumphantly conquered all upon the field of warfare and conflict he rests, to behold his victories' trophies. The law of contradictories and correspondences guides him in judging of results, in drawing conclusions from being able to see both ends of his simple staff that he started out with. Cause rests upon one end and effects upon the other. Both lie within his grasp, and are obedient to all commands.

The last external life of the embodied human soul has been experienced, the lessons learned, the fruits of good and evil partaken of and fully accepted as the Divine Fiat of God; "Man, know thyself, and thus know thy God."

As the warrior steps from the last rung of the exoteric onto the first rung of the esoteric ladder his works do follow him, and these will constitute the enemies and friends of the new battle ground in another sphere. But when he consciously realizes which are the illusions and delusions, that which is mortal from the immortal, the seeming from the real, then all foes are put to Right and he henceforth dwells in the land of realities.

The mists of the battlefield having passed away, the country lies exposed to the scanning eye of its king. He looks upon his works. It calls forth the resolute courage of a well-trained, unfaltering will to behold and to hold in check the emotions of awe, consternation, sadness and joy that would fill his heart.

His own creations stand at his feet. The children created, born and reared in matter appeal to his care.

Can his soul fly from its own creations, whether of good or evil? No. And while some may be beautiful, encouraging and divinely inspiring, others will prove rebellious, and cling as a millstone about his neck, impeding his progress in his spiral Mazy Wheel of Necessity.

Vanquishing is the next step, the spirals have become large and expansive, taking in a vast domain, for he has not been a slothful warrior. His days of traveling have been filled with an unceasing activity that grew and broadened as he journeyed. He chose to know as he proceeded, and knowledge gained expands the field of vision, investigations and creations.

Now his domains have become a mighty kingdom. His aspirations set his mark high. The Pole-Star of Truth is his goal, and that star stands in the center of his empire, and when each spiral of the exoteric ladder has been traversed with but one motive, and that motive Truth, he can view, from the outward circle, or spiral of his ladder, the center.

This Pole-Star, which illumines the whole field of battle, exposes to the esoteric vision his possessions. Is it as he would wish? If it were so, vanquishing would not be necessary.

We have followed him thus far. The veil is drawn to other eyes than his own.

What his visions are we cannot see; but, taking courage, we can begin to prepare to enter on an investigating tour of our own country, and learn its circumference, the health of its soil and the products that may belong to it.

The Pole-Star of Love is in the center, filled with the radiance that can only be seen by climbing, and thus obtain "the glory forever and ever. Amen."

APPENDIX: GRIMKÉ AND THE HERMETIC BROTHERHOOD OF LUXOR

By Patrick D. Bowen

[Excerpted from the Introduction to *Letters to the Sage: Selected Correspondence of Thomas Moore Johnson, Volume One: the Esotericists.*] By this time [summer 1886], stress had been mounting in the H.B. of L. after the TS had discovered Burgoyne had been imprisoned in 1883 under his real name (Dalton or D'Alton), a fact they used to discredit him and his movement.[152] Although the American side of the movement was still growing steadily,[153] there was increasing doubt about the motives and authenticity of Burgoyne, and by extension Davidson. The two men moved to the US in the spring, at first residing with an early member in the small town of Loudsville, Georgia, where they hoped to form a Hermetic colony that was to be the new "Headquarters of the Exterior Circle." However, the two men had a falling out and Burgoyne went west, staying at the homes of H.B. of L. members until eventually reaching California in 1887. In the meantime, the lodge structure apparently fell apart as divisions arose in the American community over whether they should follow Burgoyne or Davidson.[154] In July 1886, Johnson, acting as president, held a meeting of the "Executive Committee" in Kansas City, being joined by Allen and, presumably, McDonald.[155] Here they looked at documentation that satisfied them that Burgoyne had indeed previously used the name D'Alton, and they sent a circular to members advising them "to have no further dealings, in any form, with either T.H. Burgoyne (Dalton or D'Alton) or Mr. Peter Davidson." But then, on September 5, when the "Central Council of the H.B. of L." convened in St. Louis, the same three members unanimously decided that "the charges against Mr. T.H. Burgoyne are not worthy of further attention on the part of this Council."[156] Burgoyne was welcomed back, and was even made secretary *pro tem.*

After his reunification with the community, Burgoyne made his way to Denver, the city that, rather surprisingly, would soon gain the largest number of H.B. of L. members in the country.[157] The reasons for Denver's success in recruiting H.B. of L. members are not quite fully understood, although Denver's community did possess some unique traits. First of all, very few of the members of the order there were also in the Theosophical Society, which had been the organization that connected almost all of the original American H.B. of L. followers—even those like Randall, who, while not in the TS, were friends with FTS. Another notable feature is that the Denver community developed relatively late, with the vast majority of its members signing up after June 1886.[158] Perhaps a clue to Denver's later and larger growth can be gleaned from a January 14, 1886 letter to Johnson from Henry Liddell, a traveling writer who was passing through the city at the time. Liddell, who possessed the ability to connect with virtually any city's esoteric community, relayed to Johnson that "the people of Denver are at present greatly exercised over Mind Reading and Mind Cure." Both of these movements, at least in their more refined forms, had grown out of mesmerism, and were attracting audiences across the country. Mind Cure, in particular, had been gaining popularity due to the influence of Phineas P. Quimby, a former mesmerist from Maine who, after apparently being influenced by Transcendentalism, had begun to popularize the notion that if people were to realize their inner divinity, their physical ailments would be cured.[159] It was Quimby, in fact, who had introduced Mary Baker Eddy, the founder of Christian Science, to the process, as well as several other influential East Coast teachers and practitioners who in the 1880s were beginning to spread the movement that would become known, after it began incorporating the appreciation of various religious traditions from around the world, as New Thought. Liddell not only found Denver's New Thought followers, but began talking to them to see who might be interested in both a course of lectures on occultism and Johnson's *Platonist*. He sent back to Johnson a list of names, and of these, at least one—a Miss Alice Prentice—would join the TS soon after.[160] She would also join the H.B. of L.

In fact, there seems to be a Mind Cure/New Thought/occult thread connecting most of the Colorado H.B. of L. members for whom we have found biographical information.[161] There is, for instance, C.R. Cundey and his wife, who joined the order in May 1887.[162] Cundey was a physician who had taken an interest in Platonism following the Civil War and thereafter became a practitioner of magnetic (i.e., mesmeric) healing.[163] Harrison Fitch Flower, a Mason who was known to be "prominently identified with other fraternal organizations," joined the H.B. of L. in March while living in Greeley, Colorado, a city sixty miles north of Denver.[164] Earlier that month, two relatives of Harrison who were living in Denver, Anna E. Flower and Caroline V. Kram,[165] also signed pledges for the order. Kram, in fact, signed hers the same day as Alice Prentice, the FTS who had met Liddell, which suggests they were friends with similar occult interests. In January, prior to these people joining, Mary D. Fiske, one of the most well-known members of Denver's Christian Science and New Thought communities, signed the H.B. of L. pledge as well. The only other 1880s Denverite for whom we have reliable biographical information is Henry Wagner, a prominent physician who in the early 1890s teamed up with Cundey when the two started promoting themselves as "Astral Magnetic Specialists."[166] Wagner, in fact, would become the head of the Denver H.B. of L. community. According to the August circular, the "Complete Course" was divided into two sections or "series," "Occult Philosophy" and "Astrology,"[167] which appear to correspond with the two parts of Burgoyne's 1889 book *Light of Egypt*. While Johnson's papers do not contain any documents using the titles given in the "Complete Course" circular, they do contain two manuscript sets of lessons, entitled "Light of Egypt" and "Chaldean Astrology," whose contents match up with chapters of the two sections of the *Light of Egypt* book. This fact, along with the contents of an additional circular—entitled "Circular No I"[168]—that was placed between the two sets of manuscripts, indicates that the lessons of the "Complete Course" were renamed when the first set of lessons was sent out around late October.[169] The "Complete Course"/*Light of Egypt* is important for understanding the development of the H.B. of L. after the Burgoyne-Davidson split in

1886. It is the first major original work produced by the H.B. of L. and it demonstrated only minimal interest in occult teachings on sex. In fact, there is no discussion of sex in the extant manuscript version of the lessons, and in the book version, sex is relegated to a single chapter, while the rest of work focuses on Hermetic and astrological notions. Randolph's works, in other words, were no longer held up as the focus of the H.B. of L.'s exoteric teachings. Being the group's only large work, the publication of the "Complete Course"/*Light of Egypt* therefore marked a significant turn in the H.B. of L.'s trajectory—at least for Burgoyne's followers. How important the "Mysteries of Eros" was for Burgoyne's post-1887 followers in their esoteric work is uncertain, but everything we know about their teachings and activities suggests that after 1887 they became much more focused on astrology than on sex.[170] "Circular No I," meanwhile, reveals other important information. First of all, it suggests to the reader that to help him or her understand the lessons, he or she should purchase—directly from Burgoyne, of course—a copy of James Wilson's *Complete Dictionary of Astrology* (1819). Two other books, both with a strong New Thought tinge, were also listed as being both "required by the student" and sold by Burgoyne: one entitled *Personified Unthinkables* (1884) and the other *First Lessons in Reality* (1886). These two books were authored by Sarah Stanley Grimké, a Unitarian Mind Cure enthusiast with ties to Christian Science and member of the Los Angeles branch of the H.B. of L. since April 1886. Grimké was the daughter of an abolitionist and the estranged wife of a prominent black lawyer with ties to religiously liberal whites of New England, Archibald Grimké. In 1883, Sarah, taking their daughter with her, left Archibald and Boston, never to return, as she headed to west to visit her family in Michigan. It was in Michigan that Sarah began to write her New Thought lessons, although the second book was completed in Los Angeles, where she had immigrated to in 1886. There, Sarah proceeded to join the local New Thought-influenced esoteric community composed of Theosophists, former Theosophists, old followers of Randolph, and ex-Christian Scientists—all of whom congregated around the figures of the ex-Theosophists George Chainey and Anna Kimball, who in 1885 established their own magazine, the *Gnostic*.[171]

The connecting of Grimké with Burgoyne is significant for a number of reasons. First of all, it reinforces a trend that we have seen was developing in Denver: the connecting of the H.B. of L. with the New Thought movement. New Thought, with its claim to cure illnesses, could attract a larger number of people than pure esotericism/occultism because people are generally more willing to ignore their prejudices about strange ideas if they feel their physical suffering can be ended. By aligning with Sarah, the H.B. of L., therefore, now had its foot solidly in the door of a consumer market with a much greater potential for profit for producers. Another reason the connecting with Grimké is important is it suggests that Burgoyne, who had been in California since at least August 1887,[172] had begun incorporating a new source of ideas into the H.B. of L., which highlights a trend that had been present since 1884: the group's doctrines were constantly in flux, and therefore could legitimately—in the eyes of its consumers—continue to add new ideas to make it constantly fresh. This would give the group a significant advantage when marketing itself. Most importantly, however, this discovery of an early alliance between Burgoyne and Grimké, thus adds an important clue for understanding the relationship between the two. It provides background, for instance, for Burgoyne telling readers—first in his "Chaldean Astrology" manuscript lesson five and then in *Light of Egypt* Part II chapter 4—that they should read Grimké's *First Lessons in Reality*.[173] It also offers support to a rumor that has been circulating in occult circles since the 1890s. The first time this rumor was put into print was in 1926 when the man who would revive the H.B. of L.'s teachings in America, Elbert Benjamine, asserted that Grimké had actually written the "Science of the Stars" part of *Light of Egypt*.[174] This may not be entirely true, since Burgoyne told Johnson in September 1887 that he had been working on that particular part for three years.[175] Nevertheless, the existence of "Circular No I" ensures that, even if we never learn the whole truth about the authorship of the *Light of Egypt*, we cannot easily dismiss the rumors.

MRS. EMMA HARDINGE BRITTEN.

APPENDIX B: CHEVALIER LOUIS DE B_

Ghost Land is foundational to the Theosophical literature, chronologically and thematically, introducing adept brotherhoods further elaborated in later writings. Presented as a translation by Emma Hardinge Britten of an original text by the pseudonymous Chevalier Louis de B_, the book has inspired multiple guesses about the Chevalier's identity. A companion volume to *Art Magic*, *Ghost Land* was published the same year, 1876, in the form of a memoir. The book's authorship spans the early period of the Theosophical Society, with its first sketches appearing in 1872 before Blavatsky's arrival in New York and its final section published in 1892 after her death. Chevalier Louis has never inspired a personality cult, and no one has ever claimed to speak on behalf of his Berlin, Orphic, or Ellora brotherhoods. Nonetheless *Ghost Land* is clearly a historical prerequisite for the full blown Theosophical (and post-Theosophical) elaboration of the Masters. Despite the fact that Britten later was a critic and opponent of the TS, *Art Magic* and *Ghost Land* both relied upon a network of support that included many early Theosophists as well as Spiritualists. Several Theosophical Spiritualists in Europe contributed to the character of Chevalier Louis de B_, in my considered opinion.

Although Edward Bulwer-Lytton was a major influence on Britten, and both inspired Burgoyne, *Ghost Land* bears evidence of several other influences on its alleged translator. Since its publication, seven possible prototypes for its narrator, Chevalier Louis de B_, have been proposed by as many authors. One necessary aspect of looking anew at *Ghost Land* is seeing it in terms of the sequence of the author's works. Its predecessor, *Modern American Spiritualism*, is crucial in identifying parallel passages in Book II of *Ghost Land*, set mainly in America. This volume, never seen in book form, details Chevalier Louis de B_'s adventures in America after the European and English occult odyssey depicted in Part I and the Indian melodrama of Part II. But for most of *Ghost Land*, the crucial parallel work is *Nineteenth Century Miracles* (1884). Here is found what seems to be an expression of class-conscious ambivalence about the mysterious circumstances under which *Art Magic* and *Ghost Land* were published:

> In America, where the sources of popular power are derived from the people, Spiritualism may be found more generally represented by the rank and file of Society, than among the wealthier classes.
>
> In Europe on the contrary, where the governing power centres in an hereditary and influential aristocracy, the people derive their opinions as they do their laws and fashions, from the ruling classes, and it is chiefly among these that Spiritualism flourishes.
>
> It is not claimed that this wonderful movement is confined to any class in either hemisphere. It will be found in the hut, and the palace; in the mining camp, and the halls of legislation. Nevertheless its greatest prevalence is ever with the ruling power. [176]

Eight years after *Ghost Land*, in *Nineteenth Century Miracles* Britten expressed second thoughts about aristocratic Spiritualists asking her to write about them using pseudonyms.

> Since then Spiritualism in Europe takes the deepest hold of those whose rank and station induces them to shrink from subjecting their personal experiences to public criticism, the author too frequently becomes the recipient of valuable testimony which cannot be made available, because the communicants insist on withholding their true names and addresses. "Miss E." and "Mrs. D.;" "Captain A." and "My Lord X.Y.Z." are impersonals, whom no one places any confidence in. There is no satisfaction in offering such shadowy testimony to those who are asked to believe in occurrences of an unprecedented and often startling character. Resolving as we have done, not to demand credence for phenomenal incidents upon any testimony open to the charge of unreliability, we feel obliged to relegate an

immense mass of interesting matter of this kind to the obscurity which unauthorized statements justly incur.[177]

This is quite an 1884 about-face from the 1876 promoter of Chevalier Louis de B_ and his father-in-law John Cavendish Dudley in two books. The former enthusiast of adept pseudonyms sounds very disillusioned about the practice here, written the year of the Coulomb revelations that inspired the Psychical Research Society's investigation in India. But in 1892 she was once again writing on behalf of Chevalier Louis, settling scores with the recently dead Blavatsky.

Shortly after *Art Magic* was published, Emma was accused of being its sole author. Incredulity at her descriptions of Louis was expressed publicly, although anonymously, by a fellow Founder of the Theosophical Society. Charles Sotheran, in a review for *Woodhull and Claflin's Weekly*, called it "simply a rehash of books readily available...wretched compilation which is full of bad grammar and worse assumptions."[178] The judgment by a personal acquaintance, published so soon after publication, condemned Louis as a fictional mouthpiece for Emma herself.

Emma as sole author of *Ghost Land* was also the conclusion reached by Arthur Edward Waite, who discussed Louis in his memoir *Shadows of Life and Thought*:

> Mrs. Britten has told us, in her preface to Ghostland (1) that its autobiographical sketches were "written originally in German", but as she did now know that language, the Chevalier put them for her benefit into "rough English"; and (2) that they were written, like *Art Magic*, partly in French, and partly in English, for the same reason. In the dilemma of this lapsus memoriae I am content to leave the question whether the Chevalier lived only in the second-rate and typically feminine imagination of Emma Harding because, in the universe of evidential things, there was no room for him anywhere else.[179]

Despite all the subsequent proposals, the conclusion that *Ghost Land* was predominantly written by Emma herself is inescapable in light of bibliographic evidence, and her authorship of its companion volume *Art Magic*. (Marc Demarest's 2011 edition of *Art Magic* presents detailed analysis of the text leading to this conclusion.) The conflicting personal details about Louis noted by Waite confound any attempt to identify him solely with any one prototype. Nevertheless, rather than concluding that there were no real prototypes for Louis, I conclude that there were several, which accounts for the conflicting information provided by Britten. She first alleges that the manuscript was in German, which she had translated by an Americanized German, and a few pages later writes that *Ghost Land* and *Art Magic* were both written in French and English. In the 1876 manuscript Louis is the son of a Hungarian nobleman and his Italian wife, but in the 1872 sketches his father is English and his mother Austrian. Such inconsistencies suggest that Louis is an invention of his alleged editor, but if Louis is primarily Emma Hardinge Britten, the sole author of *Art Magic* and *Ghost Land*, the question remains of Chevalier Louis as a character related to figures in her past and then-present social networks.

Other than Emma, only one person was publicly suggested during her lifetime. The first suggestion of a Louis other than Britten came in the December 7, 1876 *Spiritual Scientist*, in which editor Gerry Brown's review of *Ghost Land* included opening remarks suggesting "It is a singular coincidence that the circumstances therein narrated should correspond so closely to the historical facts concerning the Prince Salm-Salm, a person who has visited this country, is well known in England, and a profound occultist. If he is numbered among Mrs. Britten's friends we name him as the author of `Ghost Land' and `Art Magic.'"[180] *The Springfield Republican* for December 19, 1876 repeated the Salm-Salm identification of Louis: "We suppose the editor, Ms. Emma Hardinge Britten, would object to having the book classed among works of fiction, but it certainly will not be received as a record of fact by the reading world.... Mrs. Britten describes the autobiographer as now living, and her personal friend, yet we have seen the late Prince Salm-Salm named as the original; he was a noted occultist."[181]

Felix Constantin Alexander Nepomuk, Prince de Salm-Salm (1828-1870) was a Prussian military officer who studied at a military school in Berlin before serving successively in the Prussian, Austrian, and United States armies. While in the United States he married a Vermonter, Agnes Joy, who accompanied him on the Civil War battlefields. After the war they returned to his estate in Germany. He was killed in battle in 1870 during the Franco-Prussian war. Nepomuk's career in the Prussian military and later association with Austria fits some elements of Louis's persona, but there is no evidence that he was an occultist. He could not have collaborated in the writing of *Ghost Land* because he died in 1870. His American wife Agnes had a connection to Cuba, and a recorded interest in Spiritualism, both of which are relevant to Louis. Agnes also left a memoir, *Ten Years of My Life*, in which she describes the couple's dabbling in Spiritualism in 1863:

> Though I, as I said before, resisted this epidemic on the ground of religion and common sense, I could not help becoming interested in this strange aberration, and feeling tempted to witness some manifestations of spiritualism. The Prince, however, tried to dissuade me from such an attempt, as he was afraid that the excitement would act too strongly on my imagination. I therefore abstained from visiting some of those public exhibitions of professional spiritualists, but did not resist the entreaties of Mrs. Speirs to have some spiritual entertainment at home, against which good Salm had no objection...[182]

The second suggested masculine model for Louis came from G.R.S. Mead, prominent Theosophist and secretary to Blavatsky in her London years, who was quoted by A.E. Waite that Louis was the "inner life" of Edward Bulwer Lytton (1803-1873).[183] The prolific novelist had attained great success by the early 1830s, and his *Godolphin* (1833) was translated into Russian by Helena Pavlovna

Hahn, mother of Madame Blavatsky. Lytton wrote poetry and plays as well as dozens of novels, and was prominent in political and diplomatic life, serving as Secretary for the Colonies in the late 1850s. His obsession with occultism and Rosicrucian lore is most apparent in *Zanoni* (1842) and *A Strange Story* (1870), and Britten named him first among the participants in what she called the Orphic Circle. His interest in practical occult experimentation was unrivaled in Victorian England, which lends credibility to Britten's late-in-life revelation of his name. About *Art Magic*, Col. Olcott hinted that "the book does contain passages worthy of Bulwer-Lytton; in fact, one would say they were written by him."[184] Waite aligned himself with Sotheran's position that Britten herself was Louis. Stylistically, *Ghost Land* echoes Bulwer-Lytton more than any other novelist. Bulwer-Lytton, among Emma's claimed acquaintances, was well connected in continental occult milieu, and might have inspired her treatment of this aspect of her story. His influence on Blavatsky's *Isis Unveiled* is relevant to *Ghost Land.*

In a 1957 study, Sten Liljegren analyzed the influence of Bulwer-Lytton's novels on *Isis Unveiled*, and more broadly on Blavatsky's development of Theosophy. Without mentioning Britten, he notes a characteristic of Zanoni that also is found in *Ghost Land*, which is that after publication, the author "kept up the fiction that he was not the author of *Zanoni* but only the editor of papers which were left to him by a Rosicrucian, which formed the novel in question."[185] Disclaiming authorship of parts of one's body of work became a theme for both of Bulwer-Lytton's Theosophical disciples. In the 1870s, Britten took the strategy to greater extremes than Blavatsky, since Isis is portrayed as the latter's work regardless of tales of adept collaborators, while *Art Magic* and *Ghost Land* are attributed entirely to Louis. *Ghost Land* and *Isis Unveiled* are equally indebted to Bulwer-Lytton's portrayals of adeptship and initiation. In an 1877 letter to Stainton Moses Blavatsky wrote of Bulwer-Lytton that "He was an adept and kept it secret – first for fear [of] ridicule—for it seems that [is] the most dreaded weapon in your 19th century—and then because his vows would not allow him to express himself plainer than he did..."[186]

The candidates for Louis suggested within Emma's lifetime were augmented by only one addition in the twentieth century. In the 1970 edition of *Modern American Spiritualism*, editor E.J. Dingwall proposed the Baron de Palm as the prototype for Louis. Joseph Henry Louis de Palm (1809-1876) is mentioned in *Nineteenth Century Miracles* as a "distinguished supporter of the movement in Germany." Chicago journalist Melville Stone included de Palm in his memoirs:

> I made the acquaintance of a remarkable character, one Baron de Palm. At first sight one would recognize him as a decayed voluptuary, of the sort that frequent the Continental watering places of Europe in the season. Habited faultlessly, with hair and beard carefully dressed, washed-out face and eyes, shaky on his legs...He was a Bavarian. He was Baron Johan Heinrich Ludwig de Palm; had descended from a line of German barons running back ten centuries. He was Grand Cross Commander of the Order of the Holy Sepulchre. His father was a prince of the Holy Roman Empire, and his mother a notable Countess of Thunefeldt. Born at Augsburg in 1809, he was educated for a diplomatic career, and served his king with distinction at almost every capital.[187]

After recounting a 1861 human levitation in a Vienna church in *Nineteenth Century Miracles*, Britten adds "This remarkable occurrence was also testified of by the late Baron de Palm, who was present on the occasion, and himself related it to the author."[188] Dingwall comments that some had suggested William Britten as the author of the works attributed to Louis, but concludes "that both Art Magic and Ghost Land may have been the work of Baron Joseph Henry Louis de Palm, a very odd character with pronounced Theosophical and occult interests, whose funeral Mrs. Britten attended in 1876, and over whose body she pronounced an oration calling him `friend and companion..'" Although "Colonel Olcott thought that Baron de Palm was not capable of writing anything serious, and he may well have been right," Dingwall suggests that "the Baron concealed his gifts with a view of preventing others from knowing what he was compiling under Mrs. Britten's editorship."[189] No one is on record proposing William Britten as the author of *Art Magic* and *Ghost Land*, or the basis for Louis as written by Emma, but we note Dingwall's mention of unnamed adherents of this theory. Unnoticed by Dingwall but important to consider is that Louis is one of the names de Palm used in America (changed from the original Ludwig), making him the only suggested prototype with whom the name can be linked.

Two more models for the Chevalier were suggested in the twenty-first century by other scholars, to which I add two candidates of my own. In a monograph published in 2001, Robert Matthiessen nominated the German-British philologist Ernest de Bunsen as a prototype, which was analyzed by Marc Demarest in his 2011 edition of *Art Magic*. "Mathiesen points out correctly that (a) the de Bunsen family was deeply involved in Spiritualist and occult practices; (b) the nationality, ethnicity, and honorary title of de Bunsen fits with what we are told about Louis; and (c) de Bunsen's scholarly interests were similar to those of the author of Art Magic."[190]

Demarest concludes that de Bunsen's command of English and his scholarly style in that language are incompatible with his authorship of *Art Magic*. At the 2011 biennial convention of the Church of Light, Marc gave a presentation about Britten which went into detail about his reasons for nominating the Duke of Pomar, son of the Countess of Caithness, as a more plausible prototype than any of those heretofore suggested, in part because of his resemblance to a Chevalier Louis portrait published in Olcott's *Old Diary Leaves*. This relies not on any likelihood of the Duke assisting Britten directly, but rather the Countess using her son as a mouthpiece for a variety of Spiritualist projects for which she was his ghostwriter.

Part II of *Ghost Land*, provocatively titled "The Adept," opens twenty years after the close of Part I with "autobiographical sketches of the Chevalier de B_ continued":

To traverse many lands, sound the heart-throbs, listen to the inner revealings, and learn the life mysteries of many a strange people...I have something that has followed me, or rather infilled my soul, through every changing scene, in every wild mutation of fortune—on the battle-field, in the dungeon, in the cabinet of princes, in the hut of the charcoal-burner, in the deep crypts of Central India, and amidst the awful rites of Oriental mysticism, in the paradises of love, and the shipwreck of every hope—something which has never forsaken or left me alone; something which stands by me now, as I write in my sea-girt island dwelling, on the shores of the blue Mediterranean [191]

This passage describes neither Emma Hardinge Britten, Prince Salm-Salm, the Baron de Palm, the Duc de Pomar, the Countess of Caithness, Ernest de Bunsen, nor Emil Wittgenstein. But it perfectly describes an early member of the Theosophical Society with apparent links to both Britten and Mme. Blavatsky.

Sir Richard Francis Burton (1821-1890) had been deeply involved in occult circles during his time at Oxford in the early 1840s— the same circles in which Emma Floyd was moving at the time, in which the central figure was Edward Bulwer-Lytton. By 1860 he had become the most celebrated British explorer of the mid-19th century. Burton first met Helena Blavatsky in Cairo in 1853 as he was preparing for his great trip to Mecca; this at least is the claim made by Albert Rawson in a colorful memoir written on the occasion of Burton's death. In his youth, Burton was a soldier renowned for his mastery of languages, 29 according to one count. In the 1850s his expeditions to Mecca and the source of the Nile produced popular books about his adventures, and he continued to produce vivid travel narratives for the rest of his life, while a British diplomat serving in Asia, Africa, South America, and Europe. More relevantly to Chevalier Louis, Burton was a lifelong enthusiast of astrology and occult lore. Burton, like Emil Wittgenstein, was an honorary founding member of the British Spiritualist Association in 1873 and joined the Theosophical Society later in the decade. Both had provided testimony to the 1869 London Dialectical Society, which also recorded Lady Caithness and Bulwer-Lytton as witnesses. While there is no evidence of collaboration between Britten and Burton, Blavatsky's connection with the explorer was documented by one of her closest associates. Albert Rawson, who introduced Burton to Blavatsky, claimed to have made four extensive journeys to the Middle East.

Ghost Land appears to consist of three authorial voices each with a different relationship to Emma Hardinge Britten. Louis in Part One is a continental male version of Emma and the narrative rests on her own extensive experience in the occult milieu. Here Britten loses control of her narrative by sometimes forgetting whether she is herself or Louis. Louis in Part Two has matured into a much more masculine character, whose adventures and traits reflect those of Richard Francis Burton. In this section, Emma reveals herself to have only secondhand and vague ideas about India, and writes with the same combination of enthusiasm and misinformation that characterizes Blavatsky on India before 1878. It is therefore unlikely that either was directly assisted by anyone as well-informed as Burton; yet they were both acquainted with him and no other mutual acquaintance emerges as an inspiration for the Indian Louis. Blavatsky, however, is clearly implicated in the character Madame Helene Laval, a dangerous sorceress who attempts to seduce Louis and later becomes involved with a new sect in India.

Ghost Land shows evidence of familiarity with British occultism and American Spiritualism, both of which could be claimed by Britten. But it also includes settings and characters in India, Russia, and Germany; all countries unknown to Emma by personal experience. The search for *Ghost Land* influences among the Russian nobility must start with her colleague Blavatsky, but her cousin was also allied with Britten. A correspondent of Emma Hardinge Britten during the writing of *Ghost Land*, Prince Emil Wittgenstein has emerged as a person of interest in the search for Chevalier Louis de B_.

A Spiritualist convert in the 1860s, he published many reports of his experiences with the paranormal, which fits one aspect of the Chevalier's persona. Britten writes about him at length in several passages of *Nineteenth Century Miracles*, which in several cases can be seen as a non-fiction guide to the same milieu and character fictionalized in *Ghost Land*:

> This noble gentleman not only held high rank in the Russian army and served as aide-de-camp to the Emperor during the unhappy war with Turkey, but few of those who approached His Imperial Majesty's person, enjoyed the royal confidence in the same degree. In a correspondence maintained during some years with the author of this volume, Prince Emil asked for and obtained a number of volumes of the best American literature for the Emperor's library. Previous to the fatal war with Turkey the Emperor and Prince Wittgenstein both received assurances through Mrs. Britten's Mediumship that their lives would be spared during the conflict, but be sacrificed—the one to the insurrectionary spirit at home, the other to the feverish effects of the deadly campaign, into which he was about the plunge. Both these gentlemen placed implicit faith in these prophecies.[192]

While there may be several elements of the Chevalier persona unaccounted for by any of these suggested models, collectively they shed considerable light on Britten's authorial combination of fact and fiction. The influence of *Art Magic* and *Ghost Land* is apparent in the works of Burgoyne and Grimké, but hidden in those of Blavatsky and successors. This survey is included here as background for the present volume and in hopes that further investigations are inspired by the many unanswered questions.

Acknowledgments

My first acquaintance with the writings of Sarah Stanley Grimké resulted from a suggestion made by John Patrick Deveney, after I developed an interest in Thomas H. Burgoyne's literary collaborators in 2011. During research for *The Hermetic Brotherhood of Luxor* (1995) he had encountered a rumor about a romantic and literary partnership between Burgoyne and Grimké. Marc Demarest acquired a rare copy of *Esoteric Lessons* which I scanned for IAPSOP.com, and after reading it encouraged me to pursue biographical research for a possible future reprint.

Most information about Sarah in printed books is found in works devoted to her husband, daughter, and their Grimké relatives. Sketchy and sometimes inaccurate, these discussions rarely shed much light on her as an individual. The best treatments are found in Mark Perry's 2002 *Lift Up Thy Voice: The Sarah and Angelina Grimké Family's Journey From Slaveholders to Civil Rights Leaders* (New York; Penguin, 2002), Dickson B. Bruce's biography of her husband, *Archibald Grimké: Portrait of a Black Independent* (Baton Rouge: LSU Press, 1993) and the *Selected Works of Angelina Weld Grimké* (Carolivia Herron, ed., The Schomburg Library of 19th Century Black Women Writers, New York: Oxford University Press, 1991.) Reading these works led me to visit the Moorland-Spingarn Research Center at Howard University, which holds a large collection of the correspondence of Archibald and Angelina including the only known letters from Sarah and several about her from her father Moses Stanley and family friends Frances Pillsbury and Emma Austin Tolles. I am very grateful to my friend Marvin T. Jones for his hospitality in Washington and for accompanying me to Howard in 2012 and 2014, where we were welcomed by Chief Librarian and Curator JoEllen el-Bashir, Senior Archivist Ida Jones, and Library Technician Richard Jenkins. In two visits to the Center we found the staff most helpful, and the correspondence a gold mine of valuable information about Sarah and her family.

Only when Patrick D. Bowen transcribed the correspondence of Thomas Moore Johnson now published in *Letters to the Sage, Volume One* did I learn of evidence concerning Grimké's involvement in the Hermetic Brotherhood of Luxor. Burgoyne's letters reveal that Grimké's two series of lessons, *Personified Unthinkables* and *First Lessons in Reality*, became required reading for members almost immediately after she joined the order. Patrick learned of the existence of the Mary Baker Eddy Library Fellowship program and encouraged me to apply for a residence exploring the associates and influences of Grimké's time in Boston. While the periodicals and books of the collections were very helpful, the most illuminating resources for my purpose were Eddy's incoming and outgoing correspondence and the early organizational records of the Christian Scientist Association. It would have been impossible to make any headway in understanding the role of Elizabeth Stuart in disrupting Sarah's marriage without the letters preserved at the Mary Baker Eddy Library. Helping me with research in the collections were Mike Davis, Kurt Morris, and Mark Montgomery, under direction of Senior Research Archivist Judy Huenneke. I thank Patrick for encouraging me to apply, and the Fellowship program for awarding me a three week residence. Mitch Horowitz, who had used the collections for research on New Thought history and reported it as a positive experience in his book *One Simple Idea*, kindly wrote me a letter of recommendation as did Jeffrey Lavoie, author of two scholarly books discussing Spiritualism and Theosophy. During research in Boston I examined Unitarian Church records involving Cyrus Bartol and the Weld family at the Andover-Harvard Theological Library, with the assistance of Jessica Suarez, Curator of Manuscripts and Archives. Equally helpful at the Howard Gotlieb Archival Research Center at Boston University was Katherine Kominis, Assistant Director for Rare Books. I thank the Moorland-Spingarn Center for permission to reproduce photographs of Archibald and Angelina, and the Bentley Library at the University of Michigan for permission to reproduce Sarah's carte de visite. As this volume was being prepared for publication, I benefited from advice from Bas Jacobs on the ongoing Zanoni and Chevalier Louis inquiries.

ENDNOTES

1 President's Annual Report, 1878, Boston University

2 John Alfred Faulkner, American Journal of Theology, July 1, 1910, 422-425

3 Archibald H. Grimké papers, Series A, Box 1, Folder 5, Manuscript Division, Moorland Spingarn Research Center, Howard University

4 Robert Abzug, Passionate Liberator (New York and Oxford: Oxford University Press, 1980), 103

5 Ibid, 154, 137

6 Ibid, 230

7 Mark Perry, Lift Up thy Voice (New York, Viking, 2001) 26

8 Angelina Weld Grimké, "Biographical of Archibald H. Grimké," Collected Works, 431

9 Archibald H. Grimké papers, Series A, Box 39-1, Folder 5, Manuscript Division, Moorland-Spingarn Research Center, Howard University

10 Ibid, Series C, Box 39-3, Folder 76

11 Bronson Alcott to Eddy, January 17, 1876 (SF-Alcott, Bronson)

12 Bronson Alcott to Eddy, January 30, 1876 (SF Alcott, Bronson)

13 Journals of Bronson Alcott, Odell Shepard, ed. (Boston: Little, Brown, 1938), 465

14 Ibid, 487

15 Ibid, 489-90

16 C.A. Bartol, "Mind Cure," Christian Science Journal, December 1884

17 Early Organizational Records, Christian Scientist Association, Mary Baker Eddy Library, EOR 10.03

18 Horatio Dresser, History of the New Thought Movement (New York: Crowell), 138

19 Stephen Gottschalk, Emergence of Christian Science in American Religious Life (Berkeley, University of California Press, 1973), 208

20 Ibid

21 Robert Peel, Christian Science (R.H. Sommer, 1980), 105

22 Philip Gura, American Transcendentalism (New York: Hill and Wang, 2007), 274

23 Calvin Frye, Undated note, Accession A11065

24 "A Late Letter," Christian Science Journal, December 1884

25 American Religious Liberalism, Leigh E. Schmidt and Sally M. Promey, eds. (Bloomington, Indiana University Press, 2012), 82

26 Columbia Literary History of the United States, Emory Elliott, gen. ed. (New York: Columbia University Press, 1988), 374

27 Cambridge American Companion to Travel Writing, Alfred Bendixen and Judith Hamera, eds. (Cambridge: Cambridge University Press, 2009), 119

28 Sutherland Bates and John V. Dittemore, Mary Baker Eddy (New York: Knopf, 1932), 153

29 Sybil Wilbur, Life of Mary Baker Eddy (New York: Concord, 1907), 223

30 Eddy to Frank L. Phalen, November 27, 1897, L13282

31 Eddy to Frank L. Phalen, May 13, 1898, L132880

32 Eddy to unknown recipient, September 13, 1907, "for MY WILL" L09844

33 Katherine Tumber, American Feminism and the Birth of New Age Spirituality (Lanham, Md.: Rowman & Littlefield, 2002), 117-118

34"Error is possible only through the fact of freedom, or through the peculiar relation of will to intelligence." Borden P. Bowne, Metaphysics (New York: Harper, 1882)

35Henry Maudsley, Body and Will (New York: Appleton, 1884)

36 "Error is possible as a conception only as there is an absolute truth of reason and being...error is possible only through the fact of freedom."

37 "Physical causation was put aside, from first to last, by this original man Jesus." Calvin A. Frye, Mary Baker Eddy notes. Accession A11750

38 Bowne, Metaphysics, 451

39 Grimké gave lectures with the aid of a magic lantern which, like the earlier camera obscura, has frequently been used as a metaphor akin to Plato's Cave allegory. For example, H.P. Blavatsky states that "The existences belonging to every plane of being...are, in degree, of the nature of shadows cast by a magic lantern on a colourless screen..." (The Secret Doctrine, 1893 edition, Volume II, p. 71)

40 "These terms are necessarily reciprocal, or polar. They are real opposites, which do not exclude, but imply, each other." Benjamin Franklin Cocker, Student's Handbook of Philosophy: Psychology (London: Hodder and Stoughton, 1882)

41 The second of a series of gifts given to children in Friedrich Froebel's Kindergarten movement was a cube.

42 "The truth concerning error and its personification is learned in Christian Science..." undated typescript with notes in the handwriting of Mary Baker Eddy, accession A1277A

43 Benjamin Franklin Cocker, Student Handbook of Philosophy (London: Hodder & Stoughton, 1882), 50

44 These verses forbid idolatry and taking the Lord's name in vain.

45 Known more often as the law of contradiction, or law of non-contradiction, that a proposition cannot be simultaneously true and false.

46 "Philosophy has been defined, in general, as "the Search after Truth," not particular, relative, contingent truth, but universal, necessary, and absolute truth." Cocker, Student Handbook of Philosophy: Psychology, 1

47 Ernest Von Feuchtersleben, The Principles of Medical Psychology, translated by H. Evans Boyd, revised and edited by B.G. Babington (London, The Sydenham Society, 1847)

48 Charles Medici, A Prefatory Essay to the New Science: Mathematical Commensuration (Chicago: A.M. Flanagan 1883)

49 In an undated note dictated to Calvin Frye, Mary Baker Eddy stated "The M.D. and the D.D. impart their pictures of disease through a law of mind..." ("Mental Contagion and Vaccination", accession A10325)

50 Elizabeth G. Stuart to Eddy, January 25, 1881, IC 507. Arens had been the chief instigator of a plot against Daniel Spofford which led to attempted murder charges against Asa Eddy as well as Arens, after the dismissal of which there was a falling out between him and the Eddys.

51 Elizabeth G. Stuart to Eddy, March 24, 1881, IC 507

52 Ibid

53 Elizabeth G. Stuart and Jane L. Straw to Eddy, April 16, 1881, SF-Arens

54 Elizabeth G. Stuart to Eddy, undated, IC 507

55 Elizabeth G. Stuart and Jane L Straw to Eddy, undated, SF-Arens

56 James C. Howard to Eddy, June 6, 1881, Accession L09059

57 Ibid, Accession L09059

58 Robert Peel, Mary Baker Eddy: The Years of Trial (New York: Holt, Rinehart, and Winston, 1971), 87

59 Elizabeth G. Stuart to Eddy, October 15, 1881, IC 507

60 Peel, Years of Trial, 93

61 Elizabeth G, Stuart to Eddy, undated, IC 507

62 James Henry Snowden, The Truth About Christian Science (Philadelphia: Westminster Press, 1920), 179

63 Author A.A. Draper, Hanover P. Smith/Mary Baker Eddy, October 26, 1881, Accession L09677

64 Eddy to William Stuart, November 2, 1881, V0071

65 Eddy to Clara Choate, November 8, 1881, Accession L02492

66 Early Organizational Records, EOR 10.3

67 "Workings of Animal Magnetism," undated corrected proof, Accession A10422.001

68 Early Organizational Records, EOR 10.01

69 Theodore Weld to Eddy, November 21, 1881; IC 722a, Mary Baker Eddy Library

70 Ibid, Series C, Box 3, Folder 82

71 Ibid, Series C, Box 3, Folder 74

72 Ibid, Series D, Box 5, Folder 101, Manuscript Division, Moorland Spingarn Research Center, Howard University

73 Ibid, Series C, Box 3, Folder 74

74 Archibald H. Grimké papers, Series C, Box 3, Folder 81, Manuscript Division, Moorland Spingarn Research Center, Howard University n

75 Ibid

76 Archibald H. Grimké papers, Series 5, Box 5, Folder 101, Manuscript Division, Moorland Spingarn Research Center, Howard University

77 Ibid

78 Ibid

79 Ibid

80 On March 14, 1893, he wrote from Concord a friendly message about a recent magazine article, concluding "With sentiments of sincere respect and esteem, I am My dear friend, Faithfully & fraternally yours" adding as a postscript "your work on Science and Health is indeed a treasure." Parker Pillsbury to Eddy, March 14, 1893, Item 111.22.003

81 Eddy to Laura Sargent, April 3, 1891. Accession L0598

82 J.C. Tomlinson Reminiscences, note dated April 29, 1907, accession #A11876

83 Archibald H. Grimké papers, Series C, Box 3, Folder 78, Manuscript Division, Moorland Spingarn Research Center, Howard University

84 Archibald H. Grimké papers, Series C, Box 3, Folder 81, Manuscript Division, Moorland Spingarn Research Center, Howard University

85 Archibald H. Grimké papers, Series C, Box 3, Folder 78, Manuscript Division, Moorland Spingarn Research Center, Howard University

86 Archibald H. Grimké papers, Series C, Box 3, Folder 78, Manuscript Division, Moorland Spingarn Research Center, Howard University

87 Sarah H. Crosse, "To Whom it May Concern," Christian Science Journal, December 1884

88 Ibid, 139

89 Archibald H. Grimké papers, Series C, Box 3, Folder 79

90 Archibald H. Grimké papers, Series C, Box 3, Folder 81, Manuscript Division, Moorland Spingarn Research Center, Howard University

91 Ibid

92 Angelina Weld Grimké papers, Box 5, Folder 92, Manuscript Division, Moorland-Spingarn Research Center, Howard University

93 Ibid

94 Ibid

95 Ibid

96 James Henry Wiggin to Eddy, July 1, 1888, IC 349(a)

97 James Monroe Buckley, "Christian Science and Mind Cure," Century Magazine, July 1887, 423

98 Ibid, p.426

99 "The Stir in the Century," Christian Science Journal, August 1887

100 Letters, Christian Science Journal, January 1885

101 Eddy to unknown recipient, accession #A10207

102 Eddy to Miranda Rice, March 22, 1884, accesssion #V00809

103 Joshua Bailey Class notes, March 5, 1889, Accession A12065

104 Maureen Honey, Aphrodite's Daughters (New Brunswick: Oxford University Press, 2016) 76

105 Archibald H. Grimké papers, Series C, Box 39-3, Folder 79, Manuscript Division, Moorland-Spingarn Research Center, Howard University

106 Ibid, 15 July 1887

107 Report of the International Council of Women (1888), 420

108 Archibald H. Grimké papers, Series C, Box 3, Folder 79, Manuscript Division, Moorland Spingarn Research Center, Howard University

109 Discussions of reflection and refraction are found in classical Islamic philosophy beginning with The Book of Optics, an 11th century work by Al-Haytham, later known in the West as Alhazen. Four of its seven volumes discuss reflection and refraction. By the 13th century related ideas penetrated European philosophy in Roger Bacon's Opus Majus. Grimké's philosophical education may have exposed her to these currents.

110 Mary Baker Eddy described Christian Science as a means of liberating mental slaves, for example this passage from Science and Health: "Legally to abolish unpaid servitude in the United States was hard, but the abolition of mental slavery a more difficult task," 1906 edition, 225

111 This distinction has roots in Pythagorean number theory and is found in a 1784 German text, the Magicon, which was cited by Ennemoser's History of Magic and Blavatsky's Isis Unveiled.

112 Henry Cavendish had discovered Hydrogen and the composition of water in 1810, and Mendeleev's first formal presentation of the periodic table was made in 1869.

113 The Hermetic Brotherhood of Luxor held the view of reincarnation which had been expressed in Blavatsky's Isis Unveiled in 1877, teaching that rebirth ceased in most cases once the human stage was reached. Only after the Theosophical Society's relocation to India was human rebirth adopted as the rule rather than a rare exception in Theosophy. This passage is ambiguous but elsewhere we will see that Grimké embraced the later TS perspective rather than that of the HBL and early TS.

114 Of Grimké's known early acquaintances, only Bronson Alcott had advocated for vegetarianism on the basis stated here, animal rights.

115 Arsenic featured prominently in Christian Science discussion of mental poison, as for example in Mary Baker Eddy's attribution of Gilbert Eddy's death to "continued arguments of arsenical poisoning affecting the heart." (Eddy to Clement, June 13, 1882, Accession # F00390, Mary Baker Eddy Library)

116 "if our earthly house of this tabernacle were dissolved, we have a building of God, a house not made of hands, eternal in the heavens," 2 Corinthians 5:1, KJV.

117 The "heresy of separateness," a phrase first used by H.P. Blavatsky in The Voice of the Silence in 1889, was widely repeated in subsequent Theosophical literature.

118 The Minotaur was a half-human, half-bull monster hidden in the Labyrinth of Knossos beneath the palace of the Cretan King Minos, where he devoured seven men and seven women in two consecutive years. In the third year the hero Theseus was helped by the king's daughter Ariadne, who gave him a thread to unravel so he could exit the Labyrinth after killing the monster by following the thread back to the surface.

119 This passage advocates veganism as superior to vegetarianism, further suggesting the influence of Bronson Alcott who had championed a vegan diet.

120 This is depicted as an individual event akin to Buddhist nirvana, rather than a collective reunion with divinity at the end of time (or a cycle thereof) as depicted in the Theosophical "day be-with-us" or the Biblical resurrection day.

121 Oddly suggestive of the DNA double helix.

122 Ship passenger list, S.S. Manitoba, May 5, 1886

123 The Two Worlds, May 8, 1891, p. 301, unsigned review by editor Emma Hardinge Britten

124 The Light of Egypt (Whitefish, Montana: Kessinger, 2003), Vol II, xi

125 The Light of Egypt, Vol I, 82

126 H.P. Blavatsky, The Key to Theosophy (London: Theosophical Publishing House, 1889), 302

127 The Hermetic Brotherhood of Luxor, Christian Chanel, John Patrick Deveney, and Joscelyn Godwin, eds. (York Beach, Me.: Samuel Weiser, 1995), 354

128 Angelina Weld Grimké papers, Series A, Box 38-2, Folder 19, Manuscript Division, Moorland-Spingarn Research Center, Howard University

129 Ibid

130 Archibald H. Grimké papers, Series A, Box 39-1, Folder 6, Manuscript Division, Moorland-Spingarn Research Center, Howard University

131 Archibald H. Grimké papers, Series C, Box 39-3, Folder 74, Manuscript Division, Moorland-Spingarn Research Center, Howard University

132 Ibid

133 Ibid

134 Ibid

135 Angelina Weld Grimké papers, Series A, Box 38-2, Folder 19, Manuscript Division, Moorland-Spingarn Research Center, Howard University

136 Ibid

137 Angelina Weld Grimké, Selected Works, 213-214

138 Ibid, 217

139 Maureen Honey, Aphrodite's Daughters (New Brunswick: Rutgers University Press) 62

140 Ibid, 72

141 Ibid, 77

142 https://www.academia.edu/40515728/Norman_Astley_A_Pilgrim_of_the_Way

143 Asserting her independence through rebellion against what others perceived as her duties as a daughter, wife, and mother respectively had permanent effects on the well-being of others, and this passage suggests that she later felt some ambivalence about the choices she had made as a young woman.

144 Psalms 118:22, KJV, "The stone which the builders rejected Has become the chief corner stone."

145 In ancient Rome, this was the function of a soothsayer known as a haruspex.

146 Here we see a repudiation of Christian Science dualism (as advocated in her earlier works) in favor of Hermetic monism.

147 This suggests a reevaluation of the role of Elizabeth Stuart in breaking up Sarah's family based on false promises of healing her heart disease.

148 Sarah never contacted Archibald or Angelina in the last ten years of her life.

149 Her career as a writer after 1886, like that of Burgoyne, required a renunciation of both praise and blame as they were published pseudonymously and posthumously, respectively.

150 A justification of her abandonment of husband and daughter, and partnership with a man who had likewise abandoned his family, in pursuit of the ideal of "soul mates." In Celestial Dynamics (1896), "Zanoni" wrote: "thousands of advanced minds cannot endure the thoroughly artificial code of morality recognized by society, they defy it and follow a code of their own more in accordance with their peculiar plane of life." (p. 47)

151 Genevieve Stebbins had studied yogic breathing techniques from a professor in Oxford prior to becoming a teacher of the Delsarte method of acting and elocution; her writings on breathing were then endorsed by "Zanoni" in the two-volume edition of The Light of Egypt which appeared the same year and from the same publisher as Esoteric Lessons.

152 See Godwin et al., HBL, 343-74 and Randall's letters from February 1886.

153 See the list of pledges in the appendix.

154 Godwin et al., HBL, 87, 107

155 Letters to the Sage, Volume One: The Esotericists (Forest Grove, Oregon: Typhon Press, 2016), 193-4

156 Johnson letter, September 5, 1886, 193

157 See the list of pledges in the appendix.

158 The oldest dated pledge we have from Denver is from July 1887, but the Denver group's leader, Henry Wagner, reportedly joined in 1885; see Godwin et al., HBL, 38.

159 See Charles S. Braden, Spirits in Rebellion: The Rise and Development of New Thought (Dallas: Southern Methodist University Press, 1963).

160 Alice L. Prentice, TS membership, entered August 29, 1886, Theosophical Society General Register Vol. I, 94, http://www.theartarchives.org. She, along with another H.B. of L. member, Ernest Sasserville, was one of the founding members of Denver's TS lodge in 1894; see "Theosophy in Denver," Daily News (Denver), May 19, 1894, 2.

161 See the appendix for a full list of the H.B. of L. pledges from the Johnson papers.

162 H.B. of L. pledges signed May 9, 1887.

163 Frank Hall, History of the State of Colorado, Embracing Accounts of the Pre-Historic Races and Their Remains: The Earliest Spanish, French and American Explorations; the Lives of the Primitive Hunters, Trappers and Traders; the Commerce of the Prairies; the First American Settlements Founded; the Original Discoveries of Gold in the Rocky Mountains; the Development of Cities and Towns, with the Various Phases of Industrial and Political Transition, from 1858 to 1890 (Chicago: Blakely Printing Company, 1895), 4: 410.

164 "Death of Fitch Flower," Phelps Citizen (NY), June 12, 1913, 3

165 Kram was Harrison's sister; see "Death of Fitch Flower."

166 "Man's Mistakes" (advertisement), Daily News (Denver), December 3, 1891, 3. For more on this topic, see below.

167 Godwin et al., HBL, 411

168 This was written by Burgoyne and has been enclosed in the Burgoyne letters in this volume.

169 According to the August circular, starting in October, when the course was to begin, each month the subscriber would receive one lesson in Occult Philosophy (the "Light of Egypt" manuscript) and two in Astrology (the "Chaldean Astrology" manuscript). However, "Circular No I" speaks of "many delays and difficulties in issuing these first lessons," and appears to have been sent with those lessons. A November 15 letter from Burgoyne notes that the second round of lessons was currently being sent out, so we can assume that the first round appeared in late October or early November.

170 We do know, nevertheless, that the "Mysteries of Eros" was being sent to members as late as May 1888; see Wagner to Johnson, May 20, 1888.

171 Sarah was only tangentially connected to the Gnostic. As a member of the Los Angeles H.B. of L., she had contact with Louise Off, a Theosophist who contributed to the Gnostic. Also, the former follower of Randolph in this community was Dowd, who was also a member of the H.B. of L. by that point. Finally, while in California, Sarah was friends with Miranda R. Rice, another former Christian Scientist, who was living in San Francisco and had connections with the local New Thought

movement, and even knew the New Thought/H.B. of L. member Mary D. Fiske from Denver. See Johnson's forthcoming work for more details.

172 We know this from the fact that his September 4 letter to Johnson uses a California address.

173 In the 1889 version, it is on page 202; in the 1963 version, it is on page 228.

174 C.C. Zain [Elbert Benjamine], Laws of Occultism: Inner Plane Theory and the Fundamentals of Psychic Phenomena, Rev. 2nd ed. (Los Angeles: Church of Light, [1926] 1994), 156. This section of the Light of Egypt corresponded with the "Astrology" section in the "Complete Course."

175 Burgoyne to Johnson, September 4, 1887.

176 Nineteenth Century Miracles, 91

177 Ibid.

178 Charles Sotheran, "The Kobolds Have Come," Woodhull and Claflin's Weekly, April 22, 1876

179 A.E. Waite, Shadows of My Life and Thought, (London: Selwyn and Blount, 1938) 71

180 E. Gerry Brown, Ghost Land review, Spiritual Scientist, December 19, 1876

181 Springfield Republican, December 19, 1876

182 Agnes, Princess Salm-Salm, Ten Years of My Life (New York: Worthington, 1877) 61

183 Waite, Shadows of My Life and Thought, 71

184 Henry Steel Olcott, Old Diary Leaves Vol. 1, 89

185 Sten Liljegren, Bulwer-Lytton's Novels and Isis Unveiled, (Cambridge: Harvard University Press,1957) 56

186 H.P. Blavatsky, Letters of H.P Blavatsky, Vol. I, (Wheaton: Theosophical Publishing House, 2003), 202

187 Melville Stone, Fifty Years a Journalist, (New York: Doubleday, Page, 1921), 39

188 Emma Hardinge Britten, Nineteenth Century Miracles (New York, Lovell, 1884), 33

189 E.J. Dingwall, introduction to Modern American Spiritualism (New York, University Books, 1970), xvi

190 Emma Hardinge Britten, Art Magic (Forest Grove, Oregon, Typhon Press, 2011), xl

191 Emma Hardinge Britten, Ghost Land (Chicago: Progressive Thinker, 1909), 234

192 Britten, Nineteenth Century Miracles, 351

Made in the USA
Coppell, TX
21 October 2020